Oasis of Hope

*Encouragement during
Chronic Illness and Pain*

Compiled By Susan Sage

Oasis of Hope
Encouragement during Chronic Illness and Pain

———————————————————————————————

Copyright © 2023 Susan Sage

Published by: Empowered With Hope | Susan Sage

Edited by: Tisha Martin Editorial, LLC

Cover Design: Kristina Conatser | Captured by KC Designs

Calligraphy Art by: Jeanette Hanscome

Paperback ISBN: 979-8-218-19449-9

Digital Format ISBN: 979-8-218-19845-9

DEDICATION

To the reader who feels alone in their chronic
illness or pain journey.

To my Lord and Savior, who taught me to trust Him with
every breath and for every ounce of strength.
May His will be done.

To each family member and friend who has given support
through illness and pain.

ACKNOWLEDGMENTS

Numerous people have been part of the birthing of this book. Some shared their hearts in the devotions written and those who prayed the process through to the end.

Julie, Melanie, Anu, Jodine, Lauri, and Sharon, who walked with me as I learned, then wrote and prayed as the manuscript came into being. No words could express my level of appreciation for Tisha and Kristina who worked tirelessly to help me get this book into the world.

Many friends and loved ones provided encouragement and support along the way as well. So, I do not miss anyone, I simply give my thanks as a whole.

My husband cheered me on through the entire process.

Most of all to my precious Almighty God Who placed this dream in my heart and would not let me rest until completion. I owe everything to Him. Until He takes me home, I will praise Him with every breath.

This book is a work of love and understanding. With that in mind, the proceeds from the sale of the book will be shared to help other writers with chronic illness and pain. Because everyone needs encouragement and hope. **Romans 15:13.**

FOREWORD

This devotional is written as a reminder of hope to those who live with chronic illness and pain. We have been called to walk a long, difficult road. At times it's comforting to know someone else identifies with what we deal with daily. Unfortunately, we can't set aside the health issues that impact life. The authors who have shared their hearts through the words in these devotions understand.

This book is for you. None of us wants a reminder of our health challenges every single day. Although some of the thoughts offered are about chronic illness, not all of them are. I hope you find encouragement for the journey God has called you.

I pray each reader will remember how God carries us amid the darkest night. Today's challenges equal tomorrow's strengths as we allow God to work all things for His glory.

May God's grace flow in and through you each moment of the day. May you find encouragement and an Oasis of Hope as He walks with you.

Blessed be the God and Father of our Lord Jesus Christ, the Father of mercies and God of all comfort, who comforts us in all our affliction so that we will be able to comfort those who are in any affliction with the comfort with which we ourselves are comforted by God.
1 Corinthians 1:3–4 NASB

Table of Contents

Table of Contents

Table of Contents

HOLDING ON TO HOPE

Let us hold fast the confession of our hope without wavering,
for He who promised is faithful.
Hebrews 10:23 NASB

When pressure builds, pain and illness rage, or circumstances change whatever normal once looked like, it can be difficult to hold onto hope. It can also be challenging to cling to when unanswered questions loom or there's no end in sight to the current battle.

As believers, we want to keep focused on God's promises while we wait for test results. We try to trust Him when devastation looms. But at times, the realities of how we feel at the moment of bad news may not be very close to the spiritual discipline of hope we wish we had.

Many people have said, "Never lose hope." Why? Because without hope we lose sight of God's presence, His sovereignty, and His plan for His Kingdom. We bow before His sovereignty when we believe He is good (Psalm 27:13) no matter.

We experience His presence as we trust He has a purpose and will protect us from, carry us through, or rescue us out of the hardship (Psalm 62:5–8). We are part of His plan as we continue holding on, even when we feel we have no more strength (Psalm 119:28; Isaiah 40:29).

Have you ever noticed how many Scripture verses say to be strong, courageous, and not afraid? God gave us these reminders because He knew how difficult life would be. But He also promised to remain with us (Isaiah 41:10; John 10:28–29). And in Him, we have hope because He cannot go against His Word (Titus 1:2).

Hope is the prayer our hearts whisper when it feels like there's nothing left. Hope is a connection to God as we cling to this truth. He will see us through every moment for He is faithful (Exodus 34:6).

Spend a few moments reading the verses in this devotion. Ask God to secure your hope in Him. Let your heart whisper words of hope and trust to the One holding you.

~ Susan Sage

——— *Notes & Prayers* ———

ABOUNDING GRACE

The Lord is merciful and gracious, slow to anger
and abounding in steadfast love.
Psalm 103:8 ESV

Few would disagree that one of the many blessings bestowed upon us by God is His willingness to provide abounding grace. Grace is what delivers new life, transferred by the forgiveness of our sins and the renewal of our minds and hearts. It is a spontaneous gift from God to His people. Yet it is our job to recognize it when it finds and welcomes us each day.

Ironically, the best place to see grace abound is in our messiness, trials, and challenges. It shows up when a neighbor or family member happens to drop by just when we need a prescription but feel too ill to retrieve it for ourselves. Its astoundingly magnificent presence rests within the sheltering arms of another during a season of grief.

Where there are tears and suffering, grace often seems to reside in various ways. It is an organic outflow of His love into humankind, both benefiting our lives and connecting us further to each other, extending throughout the body of Christ. Best of all, grace is constant.

As the access to our spiritual eyes develops, we begin to see grace through two different lenses. First, there is a heightened awareness of those in our community who need grace. This is no accident. God often supplied us with a particular vision toward a need. We are then able to assist individuals in ways He has endowed—through the gifts we are meant to share.

Second, we become cognizant of how much grace abounds inside our own lives. There are unique, customized blessings announcing

themselves frequently. These are the things that might mean very little to another but cause our hearts to leap with joy!

When is the last time you considered how practiced you are at recognizing and participating in His daily grace? Consider writing in your journal about the times you've noticed God's grace. Ask Him to guide your spiritual eyes to distinguish His touch.

~Melanie Stiles

— Notes & Prayers —

Notes & Prayers

A BRUISED REED HE WILL NOT BREAK

A bruised reed he will not break, and a faintly burning wick
he will not quench; he will faithfully bring forth justice.
Isaiah 42:3 NASB

Jesus chose very different types of people as His disciples. Some were hot-tempered like Peter, always ready to act. There was also John, who seemed sensitive. John's relationship with Jesus was so trusting that he leaned against Jesus's breast when the disciples met for a meal on their last night together.

We can do nothing when it comes to our basic temperament. Some of us are more sensitive than others; according to some estimates, 15–20 percent of people are highly sensitive. This means a person like this often feels things more deeply than others might. When growing up, sensitive children may be told they should be braver, more like the others. This can leave the child with a permanent impression that they are weak or not needed.

In today's passage from Isaiah, we read what God is like. He does not act as we humans do. In our culture, the strong often oppress the weak, but God does not.

If we feel that we are more sensitive than others and would like to be different, what does the Bible say about that? It does not grant permission to complain about the way we are (Romans 9:20). Paul explains that all parts of Christ's church body are essential. This includes sensitive people. No one should consider themselves more important than others (1 Corinthians 12:18).

The Old Testament tells us that God's hands skillfully weave together the tiny baby in the mother's womb. "Your hands have made and fashioned me" (Psalm 119:73 ESV).

Every person is a great miracle no matter their temperament. This view is something different from comparing people with each other.

If you feel misunderstood or bruised, turn to God for confidence and assurance. Ask for His perspective on what you're feeling. Listen for any direction He may give. Then rest in who you are in relation to Him.

~ Anu Ahonen

Notes & Prayers

EVERLASTING LOVE

The Lord appeared to him from afar, saying,
"I have loved you with an everlasting love;
Therefore, I have drawn you with lovingkindness."
Jeremiah 31:3 NASB

When Adam and Eve sinned in the garden of Eden, sickness and suffering were born as a natural part of the decaying process. It doesn't mean God stopped loving humanity. Because of His love, He already had a plan ready to allow us to draw near to Him and experience His presence and His help. Even so, the damage was done, and as long as we are on this Earth, we will have times of pain and suffering.

The good news is we don't suffer alone. It is reassuring to read, "I have loved you with an everlasting love." Think about that. Before Earth was formed, He loved us, and He will continue loving us long after the earth is gone. Nothing will change His love for us. We can't do anything to lose His love. Isn't that comforting? He loves us in the middle of our suffering.

Because He loves us, He has drawn us to Himself through the gift of the Holy Spirit. When we're tired and hurting, He draws us close to comfort us and remind us of His presence. God sees and wipes away every tear as a mother lovingly cares for her child. He treats us with tenderness.

To feel God's presence holding us close is a blessing. If we didn't have any pain or sorrow, we might not get to experience all His love offers. Because of this, we can be thankful for the opportunity to go through strenuous times as we choose to let them draw us to Him.

What about you? Have you felt God's presence with you during difficulties? Write Him a letter thanking Him for carrying you through times of pain and suffering.

Thank God for His never-ending love for you. Lean into His lovingkindness, knowing you are not alone.

–Julie Wilson Smith

—— *Notes & Prayers* ——

FAITH-BASED WORSHIP

Faith without works is useless?
James 2:20b NASB

In Genesis chapter 22, we learn that Abraham was willing to sacrifice his son, Isaac because he believed God could raise him back up from the dead. God had never raised someone from the dead to this point in recorded biblical history. Thus, one can deduce that Abraham walked in blind faith. His faith was developed through mutual transparency. Abraham was transparent to God, and God revealed Himself to Abraham. Through this mutual transparency, Abraham learned that his promise-making God is also a promise-keeping God (Genesis 15:2–14; Genesis 18:17).

Abraham "worked" his faith through his willingness to completely give up the one thing that was closest to his heart, his son (James 2:18). His worship elevated his faith, which in turn, elevated the level of sacrifice he was willing to make.

If our worship is the vehicle that drives us closer to our Father, our faith is the fuel that accelerates our journey into His presence. To truly make worship a lifestyle, it must be coupled with faith.

"For without faith, it is impossible to please [God]." (Hebrews 11:6)

The true worshipper never wants to displease the source of his or her worship. Consider this: Worship without sacrifice is not worship at all because at the heart of worship is our sacrifice. Worship is defined by our willingness to give up our ideals to embrace the ideals of Jesus Christ, the source of our worship.

As echoed in the song, "I Surrender All," true worship necessitates the willingness to give up absolutely everything to please our Lord, Savior, God, and King.

Today, "work" your faith by offering God a sacrifice of praise. Thank Him for your breakthrough, trusting that it is at hand. Praise Him for your deliverance even though you can't see it, knowing that since He said it, then it must be true. Then, glorify Him for His faithfulness, trusting that He will complete His work. Blend your faith with your worship, and watch Him work on your behalf.

-Sharon Williams

———— *Notes & Prayers* ————

OUR HERO

He himself bore our sins in his body on the tree,
that we might die to sin and live to righteousness.
By his wounds you have been healed.
1 Peter 2:24 ESV

It is the ultimate sacrifice, the greatest love to ever be shown, for one to sacrifice his or her life for another. We see it in countless stories: a mother laying down her life to protect her child; a husband as a living shield, protecting his wife; first responders, members of the armed forces, and ordinary citizens putting themselves in a hazardous place to protect and save others. We are captivated by the deeds of these types of heroes, and we long for a personal Hero-Savior.

Our Hero-Savior is Jesus Christ. Jesus came to the world to be "Emmanuel," God with us. He came to show us how to love God and others. Ultimately, He came to pay the price for the forgiveness of our sins by dying on the cross. When we accept His sacrifice for us, we are dead to sin and no longer need to live with its stranglehold on our lives.

If that wasn't enough, Jesus miraculously denied the power of the grave and arose from the dead. By this same power of the Holy Spirit, we can live in righteousness, which will bring healing and restoration to our bodies, minds, and souls.

The Lord doesn't want us to return to our former harmful habits and behaviors but rather to live a new kind of life. We become new creations that can leave sin behind us forever. The Savior our souls have longed for saved us so we could appreciate the Hero He is.

Go forward in the freedom of knowing that you have been empowered to live a new kind of life, free from the bonds of sin and death. Today, spend time thanking Jesus for being your ultimate Hero.

~Jodine Zeitler

—— Notes & Prayers ——

FINDING PEACE AND COMFORT IN HIS HOLD

[Jesus Christ] is before all things, and in him
all things hold together.
Colossians 1:17 ESV

The puzzles of our lives sometimes seem jumbled. Pieces mix and shift on the puzzle mat. We lose patience, trying to force pieces to match. "Why is this puzzle so impossibly huge?" we might ask. Overwhelmed, frustrated, tired, and even angry, we want to sweep it off the table and quit. We can't understand how pieces fit because we can't see the intricacies of the big picture.

Our lives are types of puzzles. We have difficulty understanding how every detail can come together. The puzzles of our lives fit perfectly, from infinity past to future with no dimensions or boundaries of time and space. In all details of everything within any experience, today's suffering piece somehow fits into the grand puzzle created before time began.

And Who is holding this puzzle together? Jesus Christ, our Savior. His hands hold the puzzle and embrace each piece of our life. His sovereign, wise, loving, powerful, and good hands hold our future. He's accomplishing His redemptive work as He brings together each detail. Our souls can find peace and comfort, not in knowing how our puzzle will look, but in the beauty of His finished plan when we will dwell forever with Jesus in the new heaven and earth (Isaiah 65:17; 2 Peter 3:13; Revelation 21:1).

We can trust Him with our today to be okay because we're in His hold. And one day, we'll see the whole puzzle worked out for His glory, vibrant in beautiful perfection.

"And we know that for those who love God all things work together for good, for those who are called according to his purpose." (Romans 8:28 ESV)

We'll sing, "To the great One in Three, eternal praises be, hence evermore. His sovereign majesty may we in glory see, and to eternity love and adore" ("Come, Thou Almighty King," author unknown).

We don't see the completed picture yet, but today, let's praise Jesus, finding peace and comfort as He holds all things together.

~Lauri Hogle

—— *Notes & Prayers* ——

ASK AND RECEIVE

This is eternal life, that they may know You,
the only true God, and Jesus Christ whom You have sent.
John 17:3 NASB

Many of us bring lists before God of hopes and wishes.

"Take this illness away."

"Make me completely well and strong."

"Remove this trial."

"By Your name, put Your healing hand on the one I love."

We can grow discouraged or overwhelmed if God doesn't seem to act on what we ask or how we ask. Some people might say we lack faith, so God won't respond. Others proclaim we have unconfessed sin. In those times, gloom can spread and dejection may set in.

It is important to remember a few key facts.

- Jesus prayed for the removal of what was ahead of Him. Instead, the Father strengthened Him for what was to come.

- Paul asked for God to remove a "thorn." Instead, he received grace and strength (2 Corinthians 12:7–9).

- Job battled with physical suffering while begging God for answers. God reminded Job of Who He was and all He'd done.

In each case, there was a pleading, a heart cry, a multi-layered request. God's response was to deepen the relationship of each person with the confidence of His presence.

No matter what we're dealing with, trust can grow from the very core of pain if we allow it as we choose to remind ourselves of God's character.

His faithfulness never ends (2 Timothy 2:13). His love is unconditional (Romans 5:8). He is sovereign (Colossians 1:16–17). He is forgiving (Ephesians 1:7). God is consistent (James 1:17). The more we know of God, the deeper we can begin to experience His unfailing love and trust His answers or lack of them.

By choosing to receive His desires for us, we can release our expectations of Him. We can then grow to put our faith in Him no matter what's happening around us.

Spend time with God today. Ask Him to show you how to receive all He has for you. Thank Him for Who He is and what He has done.

–Susan Sage

Notes & Prayers

ANYTHING *HE* CAN DO...

Truly, truly, I say to you, whoever believes in me
will also do the works that I do; and greater works than
these will he do, because I am going to the Father.
John 14:12 ESV

When you were young, did you ever find yourself singing, "Anything you can do, I can do better?" This song spews a variety of claims of superiority.

While Jesus is the greatest of all time, His view is different from ours. In today's text, the same God–Man who healed the sick, raised the dead, and fed thousands with a fish dinner is letting us know that "Anything I can do, you can do better," as we do them in the power of His name.

What a faith booster it is to know that Jesus has given His people such authority! Today He is challenging us to choose faith and speak forth the simple declaration that we can do what He did, and more, by the power of His name.

Our faith is the evidence of what we choose to believe to manifest according to Hebrews chapter 11. Faith is a decision that is strengthened by God's Word according to Romans 10:17. It has nothing to do with what we are currently experiencing. Faith is a conscious decision to trust what we desire to see. It isn't always easy, but it is always worth it!

Picture something big that you want to do, something you know you cannot do in your own efforts—whether it be relief from physical pain, mental anguish, or needs to be supplied. Now, assuming a posture of faith that says, "I choose to believe what Jesus said," begin to make a declaration that "since He said it, I'll walk in it."

You may find instant results. Then again, you may not see an immediate change, and that's OK. Whether your breakthrough is instant or not, never stop declaring and believing through faith in His authority placed in you, then trust His timing in it.

-Sharon Williams

Notes & Prayers

GOD GIVES US STRENGTH

I can do all things through Him who strengthens me.
Philippians 4:13 ESV

For those of us struggling with chronic pain and illness, there are many days when strength is a foreign concept. On days when we have limited physical, emotional, or spiritual strength, we may look at this verse and wonder why God is not giving us this strength.

It is important to understand a couple of things about this verse. Paul was not omnipotent, or all-powerful. Paul is not saying he could do all things period. Paul was saying he could endure all things in any state such as poverty, affliction, persecution, or even death because of the indwelling presence of Jesus through the Holy Spirit. Life is hard and full of many trials, heartaches, and pains.

Thankfully, we can have confidence that God will help us to get through whatever life may throw at us as we trust in Him. Paul shows us he could endure all things because he was content in his relationship with Jesus Who strengthened him.

This can bring great hope to those of us with health issues. We can know that because of Christ dwelling within us, we, like Paul, can endure and be content in our struggles. While we contently endure, we can be a light in the darkness for people to see how the Lord gives us strength in our difficulties.

Is there an area where contentment is not strong? Ask God to help you learn to be content in your relationship with Him and what He is carrying you through. Walk in contented strength in the power of Christ.

–Jodine Zeitler

MERCY AND GRACE

*Therefore let us draw near with confidence to
the throne of grace, so that you may receive mercy
and find grace to help in time of need.*
Hebrews 4:16 NASB

Today's verse brings to mind a beautiful word picture. Envision a lavish throne room with a kind-looking King sitting on a magnificent throne. He beckons you to come forward with a look of love shining from His eyes.

Because of Jesus, we can come confidently, even boldly to His throne whenever we need. We come to ask forgiveness for our sins so we can receive mercy. Thankfully, God does not give us what we deserve; instead, He gives us His undeserved favor that He lavishes on us; this is mercy.

In a posture of awe and humility, we praise God for Who He is. We give Him our thanks for His many blessings. The most precious was His Son, Jesus Christ.

Because of the work Jesus did, we can tell God our needs, and concerns, and lift others for help in their time of need. This is His grace toward us.

Grace flows like a continuous fountain from the glorious throne. God luxuriously covers us with this grace which is a gift He bestows on us. It helps us get through the hard times.

On our darkest days, His grace gives us the strength to endure. It gives us comfort and peace if we lean in with acceptance.

Mercy and grace will never end at His throne. The flow will never run dry.

Look into your Savior's loving gaze as He gives you mercy for your sins and grace for your journey. Have you discovered God's mercy of forgiveness for the sins you have committed? His love for you will never end. He longs for you to ask for His forgiveness so you will receive mercy and grace for help in your time of need.

Today, journal the ways you have experienced God's mercy and grace in your life.

–Julie Wilson Smith

— Notes & Prayers —

AWAKE AT NIGHT

I will bless the Lord who has counseled me;
Indeed, my mind instructs me in the night.
Psalm 16:7 NASB

Many Scriptures bring comfort when sleep evades us due to chronic illness. In Psalm 16:7, we read heartfelt words as David mentions the Lord's counsel as his thoughts trouble him in the night. David also shared how the Lord visited him by night (Psalm 17:3). What a lovely thought to sense God's presence while we try to find sleep.

Could nighttime be utilized in Bible study and repeating God's promises? Psalm 1 mentions the person who meditates on God's law day and night as having delight and happiness. The habit of dwelling on God's Word influences the whole course of life. The person who spends time in Scripture is not thrown about by life's changing winds but instead has a steady foundation, like a flowing stream (Psalm 1:3–4). As we get to know God's Word, His promises have the opportunity to fill our minds even in the bleak hours of insomnia.

But for the chronically ill, thoughts in the sleepless hours are often feverish and confused. Despite one's wishes, it may be impossible to concentrate on Bible reading. Prayers may come as drifting shreds of thought. One may feel like David who said he flooded his bed with weeping (Psalm 6). He asked God to have mercy and to heal. But help was not quick to arrive. How much longer?, he asked. But then David went on to say he was confident God heard his cry and would answer his plea. He encouraged himself with these thoughts.

Could we learn something from David? Could we also say that the Lord hears our feverish nighttime anguish and He will answer?

Spend time reading David's words, especially in the wakeful hours of the night. Trust the Lord to answer. Remind yourself of previous times when God has responded to your prayers.

–Anu Ahonen

———— *Notes & Prayers* ————

WE GIVE OUR MAKER THANKFUL PRAISE

I praise you, for I am fearfully and wonderfully made.
Wonderful are your works; my soul knows it very well.
Psalm 139:14 ESV

The Lord tells us our bodies are decaying every moment (2 Corinthians 4:16). As symptoms expand, let's consider God's design for our bodies. He perfectly knit us together in our mother's womb (Psalm 139:13). What a work of art! We're uniquely created to praise Him and individually crafted to become His children through Jesus Christ, our Savior.

This means our illnesses must be part of His wonderful design for our lives.

Later in Psalm 139, we read, "Your eyes saw my unformed substance; in your book were written, every one of them, the days that were formed for me, when as yet there was none of them"(Psalm 139:16 ESV).

We can't ignore this reality: today was written into our lives before we were even born. Our always-loving, always-good, always-wise God birthed us into this world and re-birthed us into His kingdom, as followers of Christ.

Even though our struggle with illness is difficult, it brings such comfort to know even this illness must be a wonderful work in the hands of our Father.

"Although such knowledge is too wonderful for me" (Psalm 139:6 ESV), and we can't understand or grasp His reasons, we can trust that "for those who love God all things work together for good, for those who are called according to his purpose" (Romans

8:28 ESV). So, our illness must be part of all things.

Together, let's join in humble praise of our Master Artist and Craftsman. On the last day of life, "the tested genuineness of your faith—more precious than gold that perishes though it is tested by fire—may be found to result in praise and glory and honor at the revelation of Jesus Christ" (1 Peter 1:7 ESV).

This wonderful work of God in our lives is pure gold. Let's give our Maker thankful praise today.

-Lauri Hogle

—— *Notes & Prayers* ——

ERASING YOUR CHALKBOARD

Casting all your anxiety on Him, because He cares for you.
1 Peter 5:7 NASB

Burdens can be defined in many ways. Certain things can cause excessive physical output. A person shoulders the responsibility of working two jobs to help the family survive. The adult who cares for his or her children, works full time, and also tends to a parent who is an invalid. Those who expend a lot of energy in everyday life are typically weighed down with further types of cargo.

The mental loads we carry can foster stress and anxiety the most. Watching loved ones suffer, sending kids off to college, or navigating a quirky boss at work may cause loss of sleep and physical ailments which could lead to conditions such as high blood pressure, depression, or even more severe diagnoses. These aspects of carrying burdens are what make life unbearable, especially when we borrow tomorrow's perceived troubles and add them to the current day.

God never intended us to do life in such a manner. He expects us to constantly lay our concerns at the base of His throne and entrust them to Him. This activity may not come as naturally as we might think. We may have to practice with purpose, leaving as many burdens as we can with Him at the end of each day. This process truly needs to be our utmost habit.

Imagine erasing every concern off the mental chalkboard of our minds and hearts every single day. And what if we chose to mentally (or physically, in a journal) write out His promises instead? How much calmer and more peaceful would our days be?

True trust in God comes with our declaration that our future resides with Him. It rests inside His love, protection, and grace. The task remains with us to show Him we believe He can overcome any burdens in our lives by handing them over.

Are you willing to erase your chalkboard right now? What would it take for you to do this? Ask God for strength to pick up the eraser.

-Melanie Stiles

Notes & Prayers

Notes & Prayers

RELEASE

*But I am afflicted and in pain; May Your salvation,
O God, set me securely on high. I will praise the name of God
with song And magnify Him with thanksgiving.*
Psalm 69:29–30 NASB

Have you ever felt like the details of your health created a prison for your mind? Appointments, schedules, and restless sleep consume thoughts leaving room for little else. Too often, the pain, illness, and other burdens become so confining we can find it hard to break out of the cycle.

In reality, we have the capability for a restricted amount of processing space; we are after all, human. How are we to keep thoughts from running amok and becoming clouded with what-ifs?

There is only one answer. His name is God. If we can learn to remain close to our Heavenly Father during the daylight hours, we will have a better chance of His hope and strength carrying us through the darkest night.

Peter and Silas sat in prison chained to a wall without hope of release. They chose to praise God anyway (Acts 6:16–40). Paul experienced all kinds of suffering including jail. He chose to set his heart on the Father (2 Corinthians 11:16–33).

Once we establish a praise-filled attitude on our better days, our hearts can remember and seek to rest in worship on those not-so-good days. Preparation for whatever comes is one of our best defenses to help us not be in the prison of the mind in the first place.

When pain and illness are at their worst, how can we manage to find freedom in the brain fog? Remember, God has not left you.

Whisper His name. Listen to praise music by your favorite artist or try a new one.

On your well days, make a personal playlist so your mind can be released to praise even amid times when it's hard to think. Allow God to open the cell door and release the chains of thought as you praise Him.

–Susan Sage

———— *Notes & Prayers* ————

THE SWEETEST FRUIT

Like an apple tree among the trees of the forest,
So is my beloved among the young men. In his shade I
took great delight and sat down, And his fruit was sweet
to my taste. His mouth is full of sweetness. And He is wholly
desirable. This is my beloved and this is my friend.
Song of Solomon 2:3, 5:16 NASB

Oh, how sweet is the Word of the Lord! What makes the Lord's mouth so sweet is what it produces. His Word issues from His mouth. His very essence is made known as He (the Word) speaks of Himself (the Word). Like Job declared in Job 23:12, we should esteem the words of His mouth more than our necessary food. When we take this posture, we learn that His Word is "more desirable than gold, yes, than much fine gold; Sweeter also than honey and the drippings of the honeycomb" (Psalm 19:10 NASB).

You can't get any sweeter than that! His sweetness is overwhelming. The psalmist declared in Psalm 119:103, "How sweet are Your words to my taste! Yes, sweeter than honey to my mouth!" By clinging to God's Word, we draw closer to our Friend, Jesus, and boldly declare to everyone around us, "This is my Beloved, and this is my Friend, O daughters of Jerusalem," or "O colleagues at my job," or "O cashier at the store."

When we put forth our devotion to Him, we not only praise Him with our mouth directly, we kiss Him openly with our words of adoration that attract others to Him. Let's kiss the Son publicly by proclaiming His goodness to all we come into contact with.

-Sharon Williams

HEART HEALING

And as he entered a village, he was met by ten lepers,
who stood at a distance.
Luke 17:12 ESV

Two thousand years ago, there was no treatment available for leprosy. It was, after all, one of the most frightening diseases of the time. Those with leprosy were left to manage the best they could isolated from society, loved ones, and friends. They were shunned.

Jesus met ten men who had this dreadful infection. They were outside the village and had to stay there, away from others. Their pain was great. It permeated their whole life. On top of their pains, they experienced deep rejection. They lacked everything that made up a normal life. They cried out in a loud voice for Jesus to have mercy on them.

What did Jesus not do? He did not establish hospitals to treat leprosy, nor did He start a health campaign to eradicate leprosy from the world as it was then.

Instead, He healed their physical illness. But Jesus had more to give. But only one of the lepers returned to thank Jesus. That single man heard these words from Jesus: "Rise and go your way; your faith has made you well" (Luke 17:19 ESV).

Only then was he completely healed. The Christian Standard Bible says, "Your faith has saved you." The man returned to thank Jesus and give glory to God, and he was the one who received full healing of his body and his soul.

According to the Bible, being completely healed means becoming whole. It involves the body, soul, and spirit. But the man who had been a leper experienced the healing of his heart—spiritual healing—which was the greatest gift he received that day.

Whether healing of the body has happened for you yet, go to God in thanksgiving for all He has done for you. Allow His healing to begin within your heart.

-Anu Ahonen

Notes & Prayers

NO ROOM FOR GRUDGES

Bearing with one another and, if one has a
complaint against another, forgiving each other;
as the Lord has forgiven you, so you also must forgive.
Colossians 3:13 ESV

Anytime people deal with others there are bound to be disagreements or complaints. Have you had conflicts with another person? In the workplace, in families, while driving, at school, or even within the church, people can easily become offended by the actions of others. When feelings are hurt and emotions rise a wedge can drive between even the most devout Christians if not dealt with in grace.

Colossians 3:13 calls us to forgive, even when someone fails or acts contrary to what is expected of them. The word forgiving is based on the root word for grace. Grace is what occurs when we are forgiven even though we don't deserve it.

Today's verse is referring to the person who was hurt, instructing them to forgive the one who offended them as the Lord forgave. The person who is upset should make the first move in bearing with one another and forgiving, not waiting for the wrongdoer to apologize.

It is possible the person who caused the complaint may not be aware of what they have done. When the upset person forgives, they are set free from lingering resentments and can act in Christlike love toward the one who offended. This is how the Lord forgave us and serves as the model for how He wants us to treat others.

Grudges have no room in the life of a Christian. Part of being a Christ-follower is the continuing desire to become more Christlike and, by doing so, to lead others to faith in Jesus. If we choose not to forgive others as Christ forgave us, we are not reflecting the image of God to those around us.

At the first hint of offense or resentment, remember how the Lord forgave you and do the same toward others. Ask God to help you in the area of forgiving freely.

–Jodine Zeitler

Notes & Prayers

Notes & Prayers

WE HAVE A HISTORY

A man's steps are from the Lord;
how then can man understand his way?
Proverbs 20:24 ESV

We've all been there. Life looks one way on a Monday and by Tuesday, everything is completely different. Change can quickly become an uncomfortable space if a situation stretches beyond what we consider to be our reasonable expectations. We recognize when these types of challenges have arrived because we find ourselves thinking—or even proclaiming aloud, "Hey wait a minute! I didn't sign on for this!"

At that point, it is easy to take the final step into being completely overwhelmed. We are inundated by chaotic emotions and circumstances that seem way beyond our control. We may even believe God is nowhere to be found.

But this is exactly the time to ponder our history with Him. At one time, you may have thought there was no way that bills would get paid? But they did. Perhaps you thought you'd never feel better? And then things slowly improved. Perhaps you even know others who believed the worst was in their futures but saw God bring about unexpected miracles and restorations.

With a bit of effort, we can all recall previous instances—ours or those of our friends and family—when it eventually became clear God had been beside us all along. Our histories serve as long-standing reassurances that no matter how we might feel today, God is still in control.

By taking our memory lane stroll, we can remind ourselves that even though we did not know what was coming next, God certainly did. And we are reminded He always knows what is on the horizon. There are no surprises as far as He is concerned and there never will be. In that, we can also recognize He has already prepared a path for us to navigate through rough and difficult days. His only requirement is that we take one step forward at a time, listen and obey.

How many instances can you recall where God brought you through when you did not see a possible way?

–Melanie Stiles

Notes & Prayers

O' LORD, HOW LONG?

My soul also is greatly troubled. But you,
O Lord—how long?
Psalm 6:3 ESV

Does your troubled soul ache to know when your current illness will end? Symptoms escalating. Insurance challenges. Plans ruined. People who don't understand. Does your heart cry, O Lord, how long will this continue?

Throughout the ages, God's people have agonized, "How long?" Many of their words became song lyrics. These honest laments are found throughout Scripture, but especially in the psalms.

"How long, O Lord? Will you forget me forever? How long will you hide your face from me?" (Psalm 13:1 ESV)

These are time-related questions. When will this end? We remember that with the Lord "one day is as a thousand years, and a thousand years as one day" (2 Peter 3:8 ESV). We know God's perfect timing is different than ours and, for now, this is His answer even when we don't understand. But, as Christians, we know God's ultimate answer to our cries of "how long." Though our bodies are wasting away (2 Corinthians 4:16) in this fallen world, God's final answer reveals our sure future in the new heaven and earth.

"He will wipe away every tear from their eyes, and death shall be no more, neither shall there be mourning, nor crying, nor pain anymore, for the former things have passed away" (Revelation 21:4 ESV). God promises our pain will end one day. Forever.

We don't know when, but eternal life is God's beautiful answer to our weary bodies and troubled souls. Each passing day is a day closer to seeing our Savior face to face.

"Be still my soul; the hour is hast'ning on when we shall be forever with the Lord. When disappointments, grief, and fear are gone, sorrow forgot, love's purest joys restored. Be still, my soul; when change and tears are past, all safe and blessed we shall meet at last." ("Be Still, My Soul," von Schlegel, K., 1855).

In today's anguish, let's remind ourselves of our hope of eternal life.

-Lauri Hogle

———— *Notes & Prayers* ————

Notes & Prayers

CALL AND I WILL LISTEN

Then you will call upon Me and come and pray to Me,
and I will listen to you.
Jeremiah 29:12 NASB

Life in this world is stressful and not without complications. The news is full of gloom and doom. There's traffic to deal with. Social media. Hurrying to and fro, without accomplishing much of anything. Details can become overwhelming.

There are challenges such as needing a job. Bills to pay. Dealing with serious illness. Family responsibilities. How can we manage it all? We might feel as if we're on a merry-go-round.

Some people may go to a psychiatrist or counselor to discuss their problems and try to find answers. Others seek mysticism to search their inner spiritual guide for solutions. Many of the solutions we search for don't end up being as helpful as we hope.

We all want to be heard. We want our loved ones to listen to what we say. Even better, we want them to hear us and the emotions behind our words.

Who is the first one you turn to when needing help? A trusted friend? A spouse? Are they helpful?

No matter who we go to for help, one thing we can rest upon is that God wants us to come to Him with anything. We can call out to God. He promises to hear as we seek Him. We can come just as we are. We don't have to clean ourselves up before coming to Him. God promises He will listen to us.

Wherever we are, we can pray to Him asking forgiveness, seeking comfort, and bringing any concerns we have to Him. He

already knows what is on our hearts. We simply need to come. Best of all, He is the One with all the answers.

Won't you call out to Him today? Bring your concerns, heartaches, and needs to Him. He already knows. He's waiting.

–Julie Wilson Smith

Notes & Prayers

DARKNESS OF PAIN

Even the darkness is not dark to you,
And the night is as bright as the day.
Darkness and light are alike to You.
Psalm 139:12

Stars are some of God's most beautiful creations. For many years, they lit the way for pilgrimages before new technology took the place of the sexton, telescopes, or compasses. Stars also guided the shepherds and the wise men to find the Christ child. But the sky had to be clear and dark for the stars to give their strongest light.

When storms hit or clouds cover the night sky, stars can be difficult if not impossible to observe. But they are still there even when we cannot see them. Just as with the stars in a storm, in the middle of a pain or illness cycle, it is difficult to remember God's presence when we can't see evidence of what He's doing. Hurting and sickness can bear down and seem to steal light and life. This kind of darkness can be the loneliest of all, which can cause us to feel unseen and forgotten, making the darkness press in even more.

It may be helpful to remember that what seems dark as the blackest night to us is as bright as noon light to God. Nothing is hidden from Him ever, not anyone or anything.

When the darkness feels heaviest, turn on the lights. Try making a definite change in what is coursing through your mind. Maybe it would help to go into a different room, read a new book, listen to an unusual style of music, or think about your favorite childhood Bible story. Read it if possible. Sometimes, making a small change redirects our thoughts and brings a reminder of God's constant presence and care.

-Susan Sage

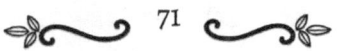

REST AND BE RESTORED

And He said to them, "Come away by yourselves to a secluded place and rest awhile."
Mark 6:31a NASB

"Rest awhile."

You might be saying, "Yeah, right! Have you seen my life?"

Life has gotten so fast-paced and chaotic. Everywhere we turn, often at all hours of the day, something or someone is competing for our attention. Television, computers, smartphones, text messages, email, and social media clamor at us continually. Our spouses, children, friends, and co-workers have legitimate needs we have to fill. Where in our hectic, busy lives can we rest a while? Yet, if we can't find a way to do so, we will burn out and our health may suffer.

When Jesus told His disciples to get away by themselves to a secluded place and rest, they had just returned from a busy time of sharing the message of Jesus. They brought the sad news of John the Baptist's tragic death. Especially in times of stress and grief, we need to intentionally seek out time alone with the Lord. If there is something specific causing us unease, we need to leave it for a time so we can be restored and ready to deal with it once again.

Jesus knows of our need for physical, emotional, and spiritual rest. Being human Himself while on earth, He had the same needs for rest as we have. Jesus often intentionally went away to spend time alone with God the Father. By example, He taught us how to live a healthy life of abundance. Part of doing that included drawing away for rest when He needed it. He showed us we are not being selfish to care for ourselves in undisturbed rest with Him. In resting at the feet of Jesus, our souls can be refreshed. By taking time away from the busyness of life, we are better equipped to deal with it when we return because we are refreshed.

Take some time today, if possible, to intentionally get alone with the Lord and rest in His presence.

-Jodine Zeitler

Notes & Prayers

Notes & Prayers

ROLLER COASTERS OF LOVE

Weeping may tarry for the night,
but joy comes with the morning.
Psalm 30:5b ESV

Who doesn't love a good roller coaster ride? The anticipation as the cars climb the first hill with those ominous click-clack-clicks combined with the adrenaline-charged, scream-filled rush of the descent makes for the perfect ride.

In life, however, the ups and downs don't seem to create the same thrill—especially those ominous plunges. While we eagerly embrace the ups, we would typically avoid the downs if we could. Yet it's the downs that fortify us for the ups.

Let's take a closer look at that roller coaster. Those click-clack-click sounds we hear upon ascent build our expectations. We know what is to come—a great fall. But we welcome that fall. Why? Because we are confident that at the end of the fall is safety. We know that after the rising and falling, the zigging and the zagging, the zooming through dark tunnels, the whipping through loops—all of which we have no control over—our feet will land on solid ground. We end this thrilling event by walking away with an exhilarating story to share our journey.

As it is in the amusement park, so it is on our roller coasters of life. God is creating beautiful stories He would love for us to share—stories of great triumphs over challenges, victories over battles, and overcoming defeats. In every situation we face, we have a great assurance that God will always keep us safe from harm. Everything He allows will build us, equip us, and reward us with a testimony of His love, grace, and mercy.

Let's embrace the ups and the downs of this season as we might have enjoyed those man-made amusement park coasters. And when we get off the ride, let's be as excited to share our stories of the wonders of God's loving roller coaster.

–Sharon Williams

—— *Notes & Prayers* ——

A MEASURE OF JOY

May we shout for joy over your salvation,
and in the name of our God set up our banners!
May the Lord fulfill all your petitions!
Psalm 20:5 ESV

Trials and difficulties are a reality. They happen to everyone—no matter how much effort is used to avoid them. Our God, Who gives us life and all the things that make it enjoyable, is not indifferent to our sufferings. He has great plans for our future but never promised us heaven on earth along the way.

The apostle Paul understood this completely. He recognized that his trials, although extremely unpleasant, represented an opportunity for several aspects of growth within his Christian walk.

Paul knew it was a significant season to learn how to trust in his God at a deeper level than had ever been possible. He actively chose to push away his discouragement in favor of companionship with His Maker. He also gave up on the idea of repeatedly asking why his predicament had come about—as so many of us tend to do. Why me and not them? Instead, he sought solutions directly from our Divine Source in every situation. He knew God could resolve matters in ways he could not imagine.

Like Paul, we can choose to retain a measure of joy with the old phrase, "this, too, shall pass." We can accept the option of soldiering through rather than falling prey to slipping and sliding around the mired down state of Why me? Things may not transpire as quickly as we may wish since God's timing is seldom in sync with our own. But we always can stand tall in our faith and pray for more joy until we see improvement. Additionally, we can imagine, profess, and declare our futures daily—whether they have manifested yet or not.

By taking this spiritual path of joy, we leave less room for darkness and negativity to invade our countenance. It leaves us free to sow into the lives of others by sharing our joy.

Who can you share your joy with today?

–Melanie Stiles

Notes & Prayers

CONTENT IN YOUR GOODNESS

You are good and do good; teach me your statutes.
Psalm 119:68 ESV

Throughout Scripture, we read that God is good. We may sing that God is good…all the time. But do we believe it? If God is good, how do our illness and suffering fit in?

Isn't this the ageless question? Satan, the enemy of believers in Christ, brought doubt to Eve's heart. Satan hissed, "Did God really say that? No, you can be wise like God. You can know what's best for yourself."

In one sinful bite of fruit, the enemy made her and us think we are "like God, knowing good and evil" (Genesis 3:5 ESV). Because Eve rationalized her disobedience to the One Who is good, all the time, we're now born into the same sinful nature. So, why do think we know what's good?

Our suffering was not part of God's perfect design before the fall that we read about in Genesis 3. His created world did not include suffering. But is He indeed still good?

"For the Lord is good; his steadfast love endures forever, and his faithfulness to all generations." (Psalm 100:5 ESV)

If God's faithfulness extends to all generations, this means He's sovereignly acting in our suffering right now, in this generation. If we believe His goodness, steadfast love, and faithfulness endure, and He hasn't changed, and what He does is always good, then He is somehow doing something good, perfectly loving, and faithful for us as we suffer, right?

"And we know that for those who love God all things work together for good, for those who are called according to his purpose" (Romans 8:28 ESV).

Let's trust that our loving Father is always good, and He works our illness together for His good purposes; we will despair if we don't. Because the enemy lies, Satan makes us doubt God's goodness. Singing truth can help us become content in those moments. "How good is the God we adore!" (Hart, J., 1857).

What song could you sing of God's goodness today?

-Lauri Hogle

Notes & Prayers

GOD'S CONSOLATION

When my anxious thoughts multiply within me,
Your consolations delight my soul.
Psalm 94:19 NASB

As you go about your day, do you ever worry over a problem? Perhaps it's how you're going to pay a certain bill. Maybe a situation at work or with a coworker causes you concern. One thought leads to another, then another. Soon your mind becomes an anxious mess.

It's so easy to get into that cycle. God doesn't want us to live this way. Anxiety doesn't come from Him. We make it worse by worrying instead of asking God for help.

Frequently, the issues we are distressed about are outside of our ability to manage anyway. By allowing anxiety to grow we think we can gain control of the situation, and we don't want to give it up.

God wants to help us. He's waiting for us to ask Him. He will relieve the burden on our minds. He can be trusted to take care of our needs. He longs to comfort and console us as a human parent would. When we hand over control, our minds can be freed of anxiety, and this will delight our souls. It is such a relief to let it all go and trust God to handle all our concerns.

Releasing the need to control and acknowledging God's power over all things, we can learn to trust Him with the things that can cause anxiety. What is weighing heavily on your mind today? Is worrying about it going to help?

God wants to lighten your burden. Take your concerns to God in prayer and leave them there. He will give you peace and console your mind. Sit back and watch what God will do.

–Julie Wilson Smith

PERMANENT HOPE

Let Your lovingkindness, O LORD, be upon us,
According as we have hoped in You.
Psalm 33:22

With all of the world's issues in areas of health, politics, race, and economics, it is not surprising that Christian counseling helplines are swamped with people who feel hopeless. Cultural divisions cause turmoil. The cost of living escalates. Divisiveness grows. Loss is great. Many are looking for answers or at least hope that something will change.

What words of advice can we offer? What do we have to give that will ease any of life's weights?

The answers will not come through medicine or doctors, new leadership, the stopping of wars, or a windfall of money. Those things might ease pressures for a time, but their help will be short-lived because we live in a constantly changing world.

The only answer promised to give hope and strength for every single crisis we might face is the same one Peter gave to the man begging for money in Acts 3. "I do not possess silver and gold, but what I do have I give to you: In the name of Jesus Christ the Nazarene—walk!" (Acts 3: 6)

It seems the man figured if he had money, at least some of his problems would be temporarily solved. He was much like the woman at the well we read about in John 4. She wanted a solution but wasn't looking deep enough.

For the begging man and the waterless woman, they needed more. They needed hope to face their situations. They needed hope that would go beyond the temporary and carry them through all of the changes they would face. They needed hope to see beyond their current situations.

Jesus was the answer for them in the same way He is for us today. We are promised hope in Him as we trust His lovingkindness especially when upheavals threaten to overwhelm us. Hope is the reward of putting our faith in God.

Where is your hope today? Ask God to help you secure it in Him.

–Susan Sage

Notes & Prayers

DO IT FOR GOD

Whatever you do, work heartily, as for the Lord
and not for men, knowing that from the Lord you
will receive the inheritance as your reward.
You are serving the Lord Christ.
Colossians 3:23–24 NASB

If you have ever had a job you didn't enjoy, wasn't fulfilling, or sucked the life out of you, you know the feeling of dread of going to work. Even when doing a job you've enjoyed, you may have had some days when you felt the tendency to do only what was required and nothing more.

When working without a sense of personal motivation, the work being done may be done grudgingly, resulting in resentment and bitterness. The apostle Paul wrote the directive in Colossians 3:23–24 encouraging honest and heartfelt work and the wise words are as valid for all of us today.

He instructs us to do whatever we do from our heart and soul as if we were working for the Lord as our Master and not for a person. The term whatever you do could mean anything from what we do for employment to volunteering in a church or community. It could also include the work done for our families and the effort we give to relationships.

When we work as if we are doing it for the Lord, the love and reverence we have for God should lead us to serve to the best of our ability without requiring an earthly reward or recognition. A spiritual reward includes our inheritance as children of God, the promised Kingdom of God for those who have been saved by His grace through Jesus Christ.

Imagine the increased level of quality and productivity in life if every believer did their work with all of their heart and soul as if they were serving God and not a human.

Whatever you put your hand to today, do it as if you were doing it for the Lord as your Master.

–Jodine Zeitler

Notes & Prayers

DEAR DRAGON SLAYER, LET ME SHARPEN YOUR IRON

Iron sharpens iron, and one man sharpens another.
Proverbs 27:17 ESV

Do you feel like the iron of your faith is becoming dull? Are you struggling to use your blade to slay your Goliath? Never fear. Help is near.

Moses had to depend on Joshua and Hur to lift his arms so that Israel could win their battle against Amalek. David could have fallen prey to an angry, backslidden king had it not been for his beloved friend, Jonathan. Ruth needed Naomi's instruction to walk in her destiny as a mother in Jesus' lineage. We all need friends who will hold our hand while we slay any spiritual dragon poised to steal our peace.

The adage, "No pain, no gain," holds an element of truth. Every cross we bear brings forth a crown, and every battle we face promises victory. Every trial we experience can produce patience, and every teardrop sparks a reaction in heaven.

So, as dragon slayers, we are not alone. We have a great cloud of witnesses standing beside us during our struggles. We have a great Intercessor pleading our case in the throne room of God, and we have a great God Who is embracing us at this very moment.

Rest in the Lord's embrace, allow His peace to envelop you fully, and know that He's got your back. He loves you.

Is your blade any sharper now? If not, continue to rest in Jesus and enjoy the peace that surpasses all understanding (Philippians 4:7). If so, then arise, and let's slay that dragon!

–Sharon Williams

DO WE SUFFER
FROM MYOPIA?

And without faith it is impossible to please him,
For whoever would draw near to God must believe that he
exists and that he rewards those who seek him.
Hebrews 11:6 ESV

In a social media group, someone asked a question: how can anyone still believe that there is a good God when He has created the tick, a nasty little creature that lurks in the grass and carries harmful bacteria? The writer had grown tired of battling chronic Lyme Disease.

Sometimes we are like little children who try to understand the big picture. It's as if we were playing with the empty core of a paper towel roll and saying that it is a telescope with which we can see into space. We see only a very slim slice of reality, and perhaps we make assumptions on, let's say, whether the world is good or bad. Or whether God exists. Or whether God is helpless in the face of evil.

But what if everything is exactly the opposite? What if God is so close to each one of us that we don't even see Him? What if we suffer from spiritual myopia (nearsightedness)?

And what if God's love so encircles all the evil in the world that even, in the end, that evil must serve His purposes? What if the whole time God is patiently waiting until every created being would turn to Him and would personally meet His love for them? What if He allows all the evil to continue only to the point that many people as possible have found their way to His love? What if inside every illness there is hidden the hope for His help?

It is good for us to seek the bigger picture. The Bible assures us that God exists and that He is good (Psalm 145:5–7). Ask Him to help you step back and trust what you cannot see to the One Who can.

–Anu Ahonen

—— Notes & Prayers ——

Notes & Prayers

HOPE AND JOY

*Now may the God of hope fill you with
all joy and peace in believing,
so that you will abound in hope by
the power of the Holy Spirit.*
Romans 15:13

Life is beautiful! However, as we journey through life, we may face pain and suffering. We may deal with seemingly insurmountable losses like the loss of a job, a loved one, health, or finances. We might have chronic pain which makes even simple tasks difficult. Perhaps we juggle multiple issues hitting us all at one time. How do we handle it all? How do we find peace in the middle of the struggle?

If we know Jesus Christ as our Savior, we can turn to Him because He is the God of all hope. He wants to fill us with joy and peace even through suffering. God desires for us to "abound in hope." He doesn't leave us to suffer alone. As a bonus, He longs to give us joy and peace.

Joy is not dependent on our circumstances, but rather a deep peace that carries us through them. Day by day. It is dependent, however, on our surrender to God. We start by asking God to fill us with the joy and peace He offers. The Holy Spirit graciously infuses us with this sustainable peace and joy which leads to abundant hope. What a blessing!

What about you? Do you yearn for peace as you are going through trials? Do you want hope for your future? God longs to give you both. He's waiting for you to ask. He invites you to study His Word in order to be strengthened and encouraged. Trust God through the hard times. Believe His Word. This is where hope is found and will abound.

Spend time today asking God for His peace and hope in whatever you are dealing with. Try writing a prayer and release troubling circumstances to Him.

-Julie Wilson Smith

Notes & Prayers

JESUS UPHOLDS EVERYTHING

*He is the radiance of the glory of God
and the exact imprint of his nature,
and he upholds the universe by the word of his power.*
Hebrews 1:3a ESV

Have you ever wondered how the gospel and Jesus's resurrection have anything to do with our illnesses? If He is victorious over death, what does that mean for our suffering today?

Romans 1:4 tells us Jesus "was declared to be the Son of God in power by his resurrection" (ESV). His power must be a clue. Jesus is fully God, showing us exactly what God is always like, powerful and sovereign, wise and good, righteous and holy.

Jesus holds everything up because He rose from the dead. This means He has the power and authority to uphold or maintain us today and every day.

By His power, He has forgiven our sin permanently (Psalm 103:12; Romans 8:1). He's broken the grip of sin and the enemy's authority over us (Romans 6:14; 2 Corinthians 3:18). He has filled us with the power of the Holy Spirit (Ephesians 1:19–20; Romans 8:9, 11). He is always with us now and forever (Hebrews 13:5; Matthew 28:20), and He gives us all we need to endure our suffering today (Hebrews 4:16; Hebrews 13:20–21).

"In the world you will have tribulation. But take heart; I have overcome the world" (John 16:33 ESV). These words of Jesus bring comfort.

But still, many days, it's difficult to take heart. On those days, let's sing about Who He truly is and what He's actively doing as we deal with our suffering. Perhaps an Easter hymn could be our daily song to remind us that Jesus's resurrection means He is holding everything up, including you and me.

"Lives again our glorious King; Alleluia! where, O death, is now thy sting? Alleluia! Once he died, our souls to save; Alleluia! where thy victory, O grave? Alleluia!" ("Jesus Christ is Risen Today," Wesley, C., 1739).

What Scriptures remind your heart of the power of the gospel in your life? Speak or sing them aloud today!

-Lauri Hogle

——— *Notes & Prayers* ———

 *Notes & Prayers*

PERFECTING STORMS

But Jonah rose to flee to Tarshish from the presence of the LORD. He went down to Joppa and found a ship going to Tarshish. So he paid the fare and went down into it, to go with them to Tarshish, away from the presence of the LORD.
Jonah 1:3 ESV

Storms are a part of every Christian's life. They come in the form of calamity and hardship such as medical issues, marital problems, or financial woes. The list is quite varied. But if we can see beyond our physical circumstances, there exists spiritual activity going on as well.

Storms can be protective, pulling us away from what isn't in God's plan. Consider when a physician announces our A1C levels indicate it is time to reduce sugar intake or risk developing diabetes. The ensuing storm associated with diet change might be turbulent, but it is—no doubt—for our good. These are the storms where God allows hardships in our lives to grow us stronger spiritually.

Although difficult, we should resist the urge to run from Him at the moment and, instead, turn directly into His waiting arms. We've all read of Jonah and his futile attempt to escape implementing the Lord's instructions. Can you imagine sitting in the belly of a fish for days? And all because Jonah judged the value of his assigned task under his own terms instead of God's. The only thing he was successful at was losing hope, but even then, God saved him from himself.

Nothing has changed today. In our current culture, we still cannot afford to live separated from God, while either inside or outside of any storm. We can always remind ourselves that storms are much like seasons, in that they have a beginning and an end.

Don't lose heart during your storm. Hold onto your hope. Look for God inside your storm! Expect Him to save you, even if it's from your own turmoil. What evidence do you see of God standing beside you in your storms right now?

–Melanie Stiles

Notes & Prayers

DISAPPOINTMENT OR TRUST

Blessed is he who does not take offense at Me.
Luke 7:23 NASB

Have you ever felt like God let you down? Disappointment with God can trap us in a cycle of despair. Those of us who have lived with chronic illness or pain longer than we hoped and are familiar with God's power know a certain truth: He can heal, but sometimes, He does not.

Such a hard pill to swallow, isn't it? It could be easy to fall into the ploy of believing God isn't fair to heal some and not others. Jesus addressed this possibility.

When John the Baptist was in prison, he sent his disciples to ask if this Man (Jesus) who was out there healing people was the expected One (Luke 7:20). John knew Jesus personally, but from jail, he couldn't see who was doing the things he was hearing about.

Everyone was waiting expectantly for the one who would free them from the rule of Rome. They wanted a savior. And when Jesus came on the scene, they wanted to know how much Jesus would do for them.

Jesus answered simply, "Don't be offended if I don't do what you want Me to."

This is similar to how God answered Job when he wondered why so many bad things were happening to him. God asked Job if he was around when the foundation of the earth was laid, when the stars first sang, or if he had anything to do with setting the boundaries of the sea (Job 38:4–11).

As we hold onto God, especially when we don't understand, we can choose not to be offended or disappointed both by what He does and by what He doesn't do. We can decide to trust His plan even when we can't see it.

When God doesn't answer in the way you hope, turn to Him instead of away. Allow Him to minister to your heart as you read over your favorite passage of Scripture. Breathe in His presence and peace. Trust Him with the unknown and the disappointments.

-Susan Sage

Notes & Prayers

Notes & Prayers

BROKEN BUT USEFUL

Or do you not know that your body is a temple
of the Holy Spirit within you,
Whom you have from God? You are not your own.
1 Corinthians 6:19 ESV

"I hate my body!" Many of us may have muttered or felt this when having a rough day from health issues. We tend to dislike what causes us discomfort. Those of us who live with the reality of auto-immune conditions, do not want our bodies to attack themselves. But it still happens, which can make us feel useless or broken.

However, the Bible tells us our bodies are the temple of the Holy Spirit. A temple is a place where God chooses to display His presence with His people. God chose our frail, human bodies as a holy place where His Spirit would dwell.

For those of us whose bodies don't feel like a very hospitable place, this can be a difficult concept to accept. We might think God would want to be displayed in a healthy, strong person with a perfect body. Why would He choose a broken body to be His temple?

But God is in the habit of using shockingly unexpected, or humanly irrational methods, to accomplish His purpose. He used a young, unmarried woman to bring His Son into the world to live among us and ultimately save us all. He used elderly, barren women to deliver children who would grow to be mighty voices for the Lord. He used a man who was determined to kill all Christians to be one of the greatest teachers of the Lord. God often surprises us with His choices for bringing His will to pass.

Though you may feel useless or broken, God has chosen your body to serve as a temple for His presence to reach the world. He uses brokenness to glorify Himself.

Whenever you feel like you are an unacceptable place for God to dwell, thank Him for choosing to display His glory in and through you anyway.

–Jodine Zeitler

Notes & Prayers

GOD'S MEDICINE OF JOY

A joyful heart is good medicine,
but a crushed spirit dries up the bones.
Proverbs 17:22 ESV

Many of us who live with chronic illness and pain have long lists of medicines to take. Often these can bring side effects requiring other medication to balance them. Some of them seem to help, some require constant adjustment, while some seem worthless.

Is this reality crushing your spirit? "A man's spirit will endure sickness, but a crushed spirit who can bear" (Proverbs 18:14 ESV)? Sickness doesn't need to crush us with bitter discontentment. This emotion can dry up our bones, the very structures of our bodies. We become brittle and weaker.

What is good medicine? A healing one? A cure? God says it's a joyful heart, the seat of our emotions and desires. Are we seeking joy today or wallowing in discontentment allowing it to crush our spirits? Proverbs 15:13 reminds us that a joyful heart can create a cheer-full outside, even in our sickness.

We want this good medicine. We read about the mind-body-emotion connection and know our Creator made us holistically, fully integrating us. We can't bear illness if our spirits are bitter. God tells us to reframe and evaluate our trials, to count them as joy (James 1:2).

Where can we find joy when we feel discontented? A Christmas hymn reminds us of our hope: "Joy to the world! The Lord is come: let earth receive her King; let every heart prepare him room and heaven and nature sing!" ("Joy to the World," Watts, I., 1719). Yes, it's in looking to King Jesus who is our joy.

In our most painful moments, let's ask Him to give us His joy, by His indwelling Spirit Whose fruit includes joy (Galatians 5:22). Let's pray, receive, and sing once again, "Joy to the earth, the Savior reigns! Let men their songs employ, while fields and floods, rocks, hills, and plains, repeat the sounding joy!"

Ask Him to fill you with His joy, His good medicine.

-Lauri Hogle

--- *Notes & Prayers* ---

SEEING GOD IN
THE SEASONS

He changes times and seasons; he deposes
kings and raises up others.
He gives wisdom to the wise and
knowledge to the discerning.
Daniel 2:21 ESV

Many seasons transpire in our lives. The most noticeable are spring, summer, fall, and winter. Then come the more societal ones like football, baseball, and hockey. There are seasons of celebration such as Easter and Christmas. These periods come and go with regularity, and we are fairly adept at both preparing and participating in them all.

But other seasons may catch us by surprise. These include periods of labor and rest or joy and sorrow. And we mustn't leave out seasons of calm and of storms. Our best example of how seasons come and go is often seen in watching children as they make the journey to adulthood. They start out crawling, then walk, start school, and, often quicker than we see coming, they graduate college and go on to make their own lives. They remain a constant reminder that nothing stays the same.

An all-wise God establishes every season with a purpose. They provide what He has decided is needed at a particular time. The presence of one season is often preparation for the next. Just as our children cannot remain toddlers, we cannot stay in the summers of our lives forever, nor do we want to live an eternal winter.

Some seasons go quickly while others seem to hang on forever. Perhaps it would be wise for us to stop questioning why our seasons exist and, instead, focus on seeing God at work in them. Wouldn't it be better to relish whatever good we can find within a season, rather than focus on its length? After all, a time will come when we will all enter the final, endless season with Jesus. At that point, we will likely no longer care about life as we knew it.

Are you waiting for one thing to end so another can begin? Ask God to help you see how He is at work in your current season.

–Melanie Stiles

Notes & Prayers

HOPE FOR THE BROKEN AND CRUSHED

The LORD is near to the brokenhearted
And saves those who are crushed in spirit.
Psalms 34:18 NASB

The Bible is clear that even those who believe in God and serve Him are not immune from trouble here on earth. Joseph was falsely accused and put in jail. Job lost all his possessions and his children in one horrible day.

What we face will probably be very different. Losing a family member is a tragedy. It leaves us with a sense of deep sadness and loss. The grief may be hard to recover from. Many couples suffer from infertility and frequent miscarriages. Their longing for a child never becomes a reality. They become laden with profound sorrow. Month after month, their spirits are crushed as they realize their dreams aren't going to come true.

Through every loss, God is there to offer comfort to each of the broken hearts. He doesn't leave us to suffer alone. Prolonged illness can also crush our spirits. Day after day, the pain and fatigue linger, with no perceived end in sight. God holds us as we struggle with our losses or suffering. He gives us peace. We can go to the Bible to find verses for our daily needs. God understands being brokenhearted. He watched His only Son die on a cross.

In what ways has your spirit been crushed? Where did you find hope and comfort? God cares about everything you go through. Give your heartaches to Him in prayer. He will not disappoint you. He is right beside you every minute of every day. He is near to the brokenhearted.

-Julie Wilson Smith

WAIT

Immediately the father of the child cried out and said,
"I believe; help my unbelief!"
Mark 9:24 ESV

Today's text surrounds a man whose son was tormented by demons. He came to Jesus explaining that His disciples couldn't cast the demons out of his son. When he begged for compassion, Jesus declared, "All things are possible for one who believes" (Mark 9:23 ESV). The man's oxymoronic reply, "I believe. Help my unbelief." He struggled with waning faith.

This father's story isn't the only one we find in Scripture of someone who had to wait for help. In Mark 5:25–34, we learn of a woman who had been hemorrhaging for twelve years before she received healing. John 9 tells of a man born blind who waited many years for his healing.

How long have you been waiting? But, more importantly, how long will you continue to believe as you wait?

People may have accused you of lacking faith—accusations that might have caused your faith to waver. Experiences like these often evoke thoughts like, Will I ever be healed? When this happens, what can you do to restore your faith?

Jesus often heals in phases and stages. But continuing to trust that He will is paramount. Sometimes, the manifestation of your faith can take time if you only dare to continue believing.

Pray not only to quiet the mouths of the naysayers but also to quiet the mouth of your doubt. Whether you have to wait 90 years like Sarah in Genesis chapter 21, or twenty years like the blind man, or twelve years like the lady with the issue of blood, the key is in how you wait.

If your faith is waning, begin to speak your belief that God is faithful by asking Him, "Lord, help my unbelief," and embrace His promise to restore your faith. You don't know the answer to "when," but rest in the patient knowledge that "He will!"

Then, armed with restored faith, wait.

-Sharon Williams

Notes & Prayers

FROM DARKNESS TO PRAISE

I am like a desert owl of the wilderness,
like an owl of the waste places.
Psalm 102:6 ESV

We are blessed because we can find many of King David's thoughts in the psalms of the Old Testament. Through his sharing, we learn that he often had to flee to the mountains to get away from the murderous intents of the ruling King Saul. David wrote about difficult phases as he sighed and cried out for help from God. At times he didn't even remember to eat, and he cried into his drink. Inside, his heart is completely dark like the aftermath of a fire.

It is worth noting what precise expressions David used. He did not just say he was exhausted. No, he described how his body felt and looked. How his mind was in a dark place. How alone he was.

He said these things out loud. He was not afraid it would somehow be improper.

When David insisted on staying before his God and pouring out the anxiety from his heart, his mood eventually changed. He remembered that God looked down from His sanctuary on high and heard all of David's groanings. David reminded himself that the day would come when he would be able to thank and praise God for His compassion and strength.

In this way, David unraveled his extreme pain before the Almighty as he reached out for God's help with a lighter mind because he had turned his groaning into praise. And if the darkness of his mind returned the next morning, he would do it again.

Passages of Scripture like Psalm 102 were written to help us. They are meant as encouragement during the times when we face difficult situations. We do not need to put on a brave face and wait from one week to the next, hoping there might be someone who would hear us or relate to our challenges.

David's habit of telling everything in his heart to God is one we can also practice. Go to the Lord. Take your burdens to Him. He is listening and ready to wrap His comfort around you.

–Anu Ahonen

Notes & Prayers

TRUSTING THE GOODNESS OF GOD

O taste and see that the LORD is good; How blessed is the
man who takes refuge in Him!
Psalm 34:8 NASB

Trusting God takes practice. As young believers, we may think placing trust in Him means everything is going to turn out as we hope. We may expect that trust is the key to getting what we want. As we mature, we realize that trust is holding fast to God's truths no matter what.

Repeatedly, the Bible tells of the goodness of God. Is He still good if He doesn't heal us or a loved one? Is He still good if we don't get the job, promotion, home, move, or acknowledgment we're hoping for?

To grow in faith and move toward becoming more Christlike, it is important to know this fact: God's goodness is not based on or dependent on our circumstances. What we're going through does not change whether or not God is good.

He is good. Period. His goodness stems from His character and amazing love for us. The level of His love is not dialed up or down depending on what we do, experience, or how we react to circumstances around us.

A difficult trial does not indicate His goodness has wavered. As we learned to trust His heart for us during challenges, we learn to see His heart and believe Him when we read His Word (Romans 8:28–30; Nahum 1:7; Psalm 31:19–20). Then, we can take refuge when life's storms pound against us. We can hold to the hope of His presence (Psalm 139:7; Hebrews 13:5) because, in God, hope stands firm.

We may not understand what or why we go through what we do, but we choose to be confident in the assurance of His unfailing love, His unending goodness, and His perfect plan as we grow to trust Him more.

Has God disappointed you because He did not respond or answer as you desired? Take the situation to Him and ask Him for strength to trust His heart and His goodness.

-Susan Sage

Notes & Prayers

LET YOUR LIGHT SHINE

Let your light shine before men in such a way
that they may see your good works
and glorify your Father who is in heaven.
Matthew 5:16 NASB

Have you ever heard the phrase, "she lights up a room when she walks in"? The ones who say this are usually referring to the outward appearance of the one they're watching. But God had another idea about being lights where we are.

When we accept Christ for salvation, God gives us the Holy Spirit to live in our hearts. He is ever-present and working to change us to be more like Christ.

As we read the Bible and study the attributes of Jesus, we may begin to emulate His ways. We will hopefully grow in our desire to behave in a way that honors Him.

While living on the earth, Jesus loved people. He saw ways to help them and show His love. As believers, we are encouraged to seek ways to meet the needs of others and be His light to those around us.

The more we look outside ourselves and focus on others, the more like Christ we become. We may have a glow about us from the Spirit that people around us will notice. When given an opportunity, we can point them to Christ as the reason for what they see.

What are some ways you can show the love of Jesus to the people you come in contact with? How can God's light through you shine brighter to glorify our Savior?

A "thank you" can brighten someone's day. Giving a compliment may bring a smile to an observer's face.

Ask God to give you the opportunity to be a light for His glory and for His light to shine bright for all the world to see Him through you.

-Julie Wilson Smith

Notes & Prayers

OUR CORNERSTONE

The stone that the builders rejected has
become the cornerstone.
Psalm 118:22 ESV

When everything constantly shifts and when we can't count on our bodies to respond, we need something strong and solid. We need to know something is firm. When bodies, medical systems, or people let us down, we need something trustworthy.

The "cornerstone" of a building is the firmest rock. It holds up the whole building, keeping it from collapsing, perfectly aligning the entire structure. Even after earthquakes, the cornerstone remains.

In our lives, we can trust our Spiritual Cornerstone as the old hymn says! "My hope is built on nothing less than Jesus' blood and righteousness; I dare not trust the sweetest frame, but wholly lean on Jesus's name. On Christ, the solid Rock, I stand: all other ground is sinking sand; all other ground is sinking sand." ("My Hope is Built," Mote, E., 1834)

Jesus is our solid Rock, our Cornerstone (Ephesians 2:20; Acts 4:11). As Christians, we can count on His grace and strength to endure today's storms of illness. He is our never-failing Cornerstone. As the song goes, "When darkness veils his lovely face, I rest on his unchanging grace; in every high and stormy gale, my anchor holds within the veil."

On the hardest days, when we experience harsh winds and storms or anticipate future challenges with treatments, surgeries, or potential disability, we desperately need to remember the Lord's past grace, and trust in His steadfastness for today and tomorrow. "My grace is sufficient for you, for my power is made perfect in weakness" (2 Corinthians 12:9 ESV).

We can believe His Word is true today, as it was in past challenges. It is important to remember our powerful and perfect Cornerstone remains solid, in our progressive weakness, and He will hold us up until the day we see Him face to face. "When all around my soul gives way, He then is all my hope and stay."("My Hope is Built," Mote, E., 1834).

Do you have a favorite song you can sing today, to remind you of your trustworthy Savior?

-Lauri Hogle

Notes & Prayers

WHEN FAMILY AIN'T FUN

But he turned and said to Peter, "Get behind me, Satan!
You are a hindrance to me. For you are not setting
your mind on the things of God, but on the things of man."
Matthew 16:23 ESV

Family! We love them, but we don't have to like the choices they make. When the disciples (Jesus's family of choice) realized He was indeed the Messiah, they still missed what His redemption of our world was going to look like. Each seemed to have his version of what needed to happen.

At one point, Jesus was forced to rebuke Peter sternly because he simply didn't understand the mission. After having been told he held the keys to the Kingdom, we can be reasonably sure he was shocked in the reprimand moment. Perhaps, in the same way, we would be if a family member rejects our "better way."

We can learn so much from the example of Jesus and Peter's interaction. First, Jesus exhibited boundaries. He obviously did not mind his disciple's explorations, but there were limits. He did not allow Peter to dissuade Him from His journey to the cross. He recognized Peter's weaknesses and loved him anyway. Despite the rebuke, He never changed either His view of Peter or altered his previously announced status.

Retaining our perspective and appropriate boundaries within familial conflict means recognizing, as Jesus did with Peter, that harsh moments will pass, while relationships are meant to live beyond the immediate circumstances. We must continue to be true to our purposes but can also be the Hands and Feet of Christ refusing to take things too personally.

As we forgive, we can let the moment pass and recognize that our personal love walk is increased by doing so. Most importantly, we can accept, in our moments of growth, that God has allowed the interaction for a reason and try to ascertain what blessings exist inside it for all parties involved.

Is there a family relationship you need to pray for today?

–Melanie Stiles

Notes & Prayers

COME AND DINE

"But Mephibosheth your Master's grandson shall always eat at my table." So Mephibosheth ate at David's table, like one of the King's sons. So Mephibosheth lived in Jerusalem, for he ate always at the King's table. Now he was lame in both his feet.
2 Samuel 9:10b, 13 ESV

In ancient Israel, people with any physical ailments were often isolated. According to Leviticus 15, as long as women were bleeding, they were considered unclean. Imagine what life must have been like for the woman with the twelve-year issue of blood we read about in Luke 8:43–48. We learn from Numbers 5:2 that by law, lepers were isolated.

Mephibosheth, a lesser-known biblical character, was the crippled son of David's best friend, Jonathan. When Mephibosheth was five years old, his nurse dropped him while fleeing in haste after hearing that the Philistines had killed Saul and Jonathan (1 Samuel 31:1–6). Despite Mephibosheth's affliction, King David invited Mephibosheth to dine and fellowship in the royal palace daily.

Like David's outward example, regardless of our infirmities, Jesus has an open door for us to come and dine with Him. In Revelation 3:20, we read His invitation, "Behold, I stand at the door and knock. If anyone hears my voice and opens the door, I will come in to him and eat with him, and he with me" (ESV). He doesn't care about our infirmity. He is only concerned about our worship.

If you are able, find a quiet place, and equip yourself with some sweet worship music and your Bible. Accept God's invitation to come and dine. After all the Master is calling.

-Sharon Williams

GOD'S WORKS OF CREATION

When I look at your heavens, the work of your fingers,
the moon and the stars, which you have set in place.
Psalm 8:3 ESV

Everything around us carries a story. God's works of creation shine so they cannot be missed. Think about Jesus observing the sparrows or the flowers of the field. Jesus made careful reflections about the flowers growing wild, as He compared their "dress" to the splendid outfit of King Solomon (Matthew 6:29).

Jesus pointed to the crux of the matter and then shared it with His listeners—God's provision. When afterward one of those listeners happened to look at sparrows and their activities, they may have looked at them through new eyes and remembered what Jesus had shared. Do we have eyes to see, that we are able to make careful observations?

Jesus's way of life challenges us. We are result-centered. We easily panic if a goal is not reached. It's difficult for us to wait when we feel we need something now. We don't even notice that nature around us grows according to the sun and rain given by God.

How would we be different if we lived by every word that comes from the mouth of God and remember the lessons Jesus taught about God's care for His creation? Still, we'd rather fret and worry than turn our faces to the Giver of Life.

We have been given a lovely environment to enjoy and to tend to. Do you see how steadily and peacefully a tree grows upward and also reaches further down with its roots, millimeter by millimeter? The moon and stars need no help staying in place.

What wonder reigns in creation! What part of nature speaks to you of the greatness of God? Spend some time today glorifying God for the lessons His creation teaches.

–Anu Ahonen

— Notes & Prayers —

GOD IS GOOD

Every good gift and every perfect gift is from above,
coming down from the Father of lights, with whom
there is no variation or shadow due to change.
James 1:17 ESV

You may have heard a person say, "God is good," then another responds, "All the time." The first person echoes, "And all the time," which receives the answer, "God is good."

The truth that God is good all of the time is one of the foundational beliefs for a Christian. Whether things in our lives are going great or are beyond horrible, God is still good. God's goodness is a reflection of His character. It is Who He is and what He does. Because God is good, there is nothing bad in Him and nothing bad comes from Him. In His goodness, He gives us good gifts.

Our human minds cannot fully understand the vastness of how good God is, and our words cannot do this truth justice. Everything He created is good. Every good thing in our lives is from God.

Out of His goodness, God gives us the most perfect gifts: the gift of salvation, spiritual gifts, the gift of the Holy Spirit, and the gifts of the Spirit such as love, joy, peace, and provision. Some of His greatest gifts are grace, mercy, and forgiveness. Each morning He gives His faithfulness to a new day. There are many gifts from His goodness more perfect than we could understand.

What good gifts from God can you recall today? Take a moment to thank God for the gifts He has given you.

–Jodine Zeitler

BLESSED PROMISE

And blessed is she who believed
That there would be a fulfillment
of what had been spoken to her by the Lord.
Luke 1:45 NASB

How does it feel when someone keeps a promise? Isn't it a wonderful blessing? It helps us know the promise keeper is trustworthy.

Paul knew he was called as an apostle, and he lived out the promise of God's presence in his life. David recognized he was set apart to be king even though circumstances looked like the throne was unlikely for him. Daniel believed God heard him, so when pressures to go against His Lord came knocking, Daniel fell to his knees.

One of the greatest promises came to a young girl who believed the unbelievable. In her angel encounter, Mary was called "favored." Likely, she hadn't thought she was anyone special, but God found pleasure in Mary. His mercy and kindness were with her. The angel explained what was about to happen. In response and confusion, she pondered the words spoken to her. As a God-fearing woman, she knew she had not been with a man, so how could she have a baby?

Mary did not understand the situation, but she trusted God. Though she uttered words expressing wonder at how the miracle could happen, her momentary response reflected her spiritual attitude toward life. The angel assured her: "For nothing will be impossible with God" (Luke 1:37).

Trust is an act of the heart even when nothing makes sense based on personal experience and knowledge. Mary uttered words of hope, faith, assurance, and strength. "Behold, the bondslave of the Lord; may it be done to me according to your word" (Luke 1:38).

Because of her heart, her belief in the words spoken to her, and her trust in God, Mary received one of the greatest and most difficult blessings of all time. She bore our Savior—the greatest Promise to the world.

Hold tight to the promises of God in His Word and what He has spoken to your heart. Although circumstances may seem impossible, God's purpose never fails.

–Susan Sage

———— *Notes & Prayers* ————

Notes & Prayers

OVERWHELMED

I will greatly rejoice in the Lord; my soul shall exult in my
God, for he has clothed me with the garments of salvation;
he has covered me with the robe of righteousness,
as a bridegroom decks himself like a priest and
as a bride adorns herself with her jewels.
Isaiah 61:10 ESV

The term "overwhelmed" can be defined in two different ways. We often understand it as a mental, physical, or emotional reaction to stress. Stress is the body's reaction to harmful situations—whether real or perceived. It rises when work gets busy, when coping with challenging relationships, or dealing with other extended, unsolved problems. Stress can also surface when we carry the burdens of grief, shame, or guilt. Too much of this type of anxiety can wear us down to the point where everything seems too much to face. When this happens, we have reached the point of being overwhelmed.

The term "overwhelm" is also a crossroads. We can continue in the same state, avoiding tasks, having physical symptoms, and experiencing other emotional and behavioral changes, or we can actively choose to step into another definition of overwhelmed. A positive one.

If we can set our minds on things above, the nature and character of God may begin to overwhelm us differently. David the psalmist experienced an overwhelming nearness to God during his turmoil, and described God as an immoveable security, a towering shelter. The prophet, Isaiah, could also look past his challenges to the point of being overwhelmed with rejoicing.

Both chose to turn away from their chaos and, instead, face God. By choosing to praise Him inside the storms of life, the truth of His magnificence flooded their thoughts which reframed everything.

We can choose to join them in the realization that God is nearer and greater than any trouble we might face or we can choose to remain in confusion and stress.

Which definition of overwhelmed do you prefer?

–Melanie Stiles

Notes & Prayers

BUT IF NOT...

But if not, be it known to you, O king,
that we will not serve your gods
or worship the golden image that you have set up.
Daniel 2:18 ESV

Have you ever had to make a choice that had the propensity to change your life? Three Israelite men, Shadrack, Meshach, and Abednego, who had been raised to honor God, faced the ultimate choice.

The fearsome Babylonian king, Nebuchadnezzar, who had conquered nation after nation, had erected a statue to himself to emphasize his power. The statue was impressive, standing 30 meters high. All the powerful leaders in the land were in attendance for the dedication of the monument. All were told to bow down together before the statue when the music sounded. And they all did, except for three.

These God-fearing Israelite men had already made up their minds. They did not base their decision on what might happen to them but on the intention of not acting against their conviction. No matter what happened. Knowing the God they honored and served was mighty and could save them from death if He so decided and willed, they left the matter to God. Even if God did not save them, it would not change their attitude toward Him.

The young Israelite men would not bow. They had learned the most important commandment given by God through Moses to serve none other than God and not to bow down to any image (Exodus 20:2–5). And God saved these faithful men because of the decision they made to trust Him no matter what might happen.

In our world, we may face times of decision as Shadrach, Meshach, and Abednego did. When everyone around us is turning from God and going along with the culture so as not to face consequences, what will we do? Will we stand firm in our decision to honor God or will we take the easier road?

–Anu Ahonen

Notes & Prayers

Notes & Prayers

REJOICE OR DESPAIR?

Rejoice in the Lord always: again I will say rejoice.
Philippians 4:4 NASB

Do you find it easier to rejoice when everything is going well or when things are falling apart? It is much easier for most of us to be positive and praise God when we're content with our circumstances.

It's much harder to rejoice when a job has been lost. It is also challenging when we or a loved one has been diagnosed with a life-threatening disease. Rejoicing in those times is much harder, isn't it?

Rejoicing in the Lord is not optional but is a command. Even though Paul wrote this instruction, God told him what to write. Paul didn't have an easy life. He was imprisoned in a cold, damp cell on several occasions; yet, he chose to rejoice through it all. We're not to rejoice just when we feel like it. Through Paul, God said to rejoice in the Lord always. We are to rejoice in whatever circumstance we find ourselves in.

How can we live this way with all the trials that beset us daily? First, focus on God. He is the One Who has allowed the trials into our lives for whatever reason. His goal, once we have accepted Jesus Christ, is to conform us into His image. Often, we learn deeper spiritual truths as we go through difficult times. Second, choose to follow God's instruction. We can choose to wallow in despair or choose to turn toward God, obey, and rejoice.

Notice Paul says "rejoice" twice for added emphasis. When something is mentioned twice as this is, we should take special note of it. We are to rejoice always. The good news is God will help us if we ask Him to. As we choose to focus on God, our gratitude for Him grows. It then becomes easier to rejoice.

Which do you typically do, wallow or rejoice? Has that choice helped or harmed you? Try following Paul's instructions. Ask God to help you learn to rejoice in everything.

-Julie Wilson Smith

Notes & Prayers

Notes & Prayers

JESUS PRAYS FOR ME

But I have prayed for you that your faith may not fail.
And when you have turned again, strengthen your brothers.
Luke 22:32 ESV

In Zechariah 3, we read of Zechariah's prophetic vision of Joshua, the high priest standing before the angel of the Lord. When the devil began to accuse Joshua of falling into sin during this encounter, the Lord defended him by rebuking Satan. In His reprimand, God called Joshua "a brand plucked from the fire" (Zechariah 3:2). From then on, the fire that Joshua was plucked from was gone.

Sometimes the fires of life may leave us feeling charred, and other times, burned beyond recognition. These fires sometimes create opportunities to fall into temptation. But the same Lord Who rebuked the devil on Joshua's behalf is also rebuking the enemy on our behalf.

God has given us the authority to tread on serpents and scorpions, and over every bit of the enemy's power, along with the promise that nothing will hurt us (Luke 10:19). Thus, we can rest in the knowledge that our weakness or temptation does not define us.

Just as Jesus prayed for Peter, who would soon deny Him three times, He is praying for us. Embrace the knowledge that we have our very own personal Intercessor (Romans 8:34).

Allow Him to plead your case, and praise Him for faithfully standing in the courtroom of God, defending you at this very moment. Allow Him to wash you thoroughly and reposition you to right standing in God's Kingdom.

Pray this simple prayer as you surrender every burden to the Lord:

Lord Jesus, thank You for being my Intercessor, pleading my case daily despite my faults and failures. Please forgive me for the things I have done that offend You. Thank You for washing me clean with Your blood and restoring me to my rightful position in Your Kingdom, in Jesus's name, amen.

Take some time to praise and adore Him for refreshing and renewal as you welcome the fact that He has and is still praying for you.

–Sharon Williams

Notes & Prayers

Notes & Prayers

MAKE KNOWN HIS DEEDS

Oh give thanks to the LORD; call upon His name;
Make known His deeds among the peoples!
1 Chronicles 16:8 ESV

People say attending memorial services is part of getting older, as those we've known for a time will pass on with greater frequency. While we know we will see many of our loved ones in heaven, it is still difficult to say goodbye. In many services, a common theme might be celebrating the life and accomplishments of the person who has passed away. Similarly, a retirement celebration honors the retiree for all they have done in their career. It is a special time to intentionally respect the value of this person who is beginning a new season of life. Recounting one's life and accomplishments is an important way to pay tribute.

While it is so easy for us to honor the people in our lives, how much more should we give testimony and celebrate all God has done, which is far greater than any person has ever done. The Bible encourages us to proclaim the greatness of the Lord so the whole world will know of His greatness.

The evidence of what God has done is displayed around us. We can look at our own lives or the lives of others to see God's mighty hand at work. We can turn to nature and appreciate the beauty and mystery of His creation. In the Bible, we find story after story of how the Lord has intervened for good in the lives of countless men, women, and children.

God's works and wonders are everywhere if we will but look and acknowledge them. Throughout your day, take time to write down as many of the things God has done as you can see and remember, then give Him thanks.

-Jodine Zeitler

REJOICE, THE LORD IS KING!

The LORD sends forth from Zion your mighty scepter.
Rule in the midst of your enemies!
Psalm 110:2 ESV

Are there days when it seems enemies have taken over? When we feel attacked on every side, playing whack-a-mole with symptoms, wrestling with this fallen world's systems and destructive words and ways, or when we feel like the enemy must be ruling everything?

But Who is the ruling and reigning King? "The LORD has established his throne in the heavens, and his kingdom rules over all" (Psalm 103:19 ESV). "Jesus is far above all rule and authority and power and dominion, and above every name that is named, not only in this age but also in the one to come" (Ephesians 1:21 ESV).

The Alpha and Omega (Revelation 1:8) is reigning right now, ruling over all, including the prowling enemy whose power is subject to God's authority. We do feel attacks, wrestling with anxiety, pain, and sorrow. But the "King of kings and Lord of lords" (1 Timothy 6:15) has not left His throne for a moment.

We can walk through each attack freed from fear, knowing our beloved Savior has full authority over the situation, as He accomplishes His redemptive Kingdom work in and through it.

Singing hymns and songs that praise the Lord can empower our hearts and protect our minds against the attacks of our enemy.

"Rejoice, the Lord is King: your Lord and King adore! Rejoice, give thanks, and sing, and triumph evermore. Jesus the Savior reigns, the God of truth and love; when he had purged our stains, he took his seat above. His kingdom cannot fail, he rules o'er earth and heav'n; the keys of death and hell are to our Jesus giv'n. He sits at God's right hand till all his foes submit, and bow to his command, and fall beneath his feet. Lift up your heart, lift up your voice! Rejoice, again I say, rejoice!" ("Rejoice, the Lord Is King," Wesley, C., 1744).

No matter your situation, will you join in praising our ruling King today?

-Lauri Hogle

Notes & Prayers

NONE BUT GOD

For from days of old they have not heard or perceived by ear,
Nor has the eye seen a God besides You,
Who acts in behalf of the one who waits for Him.
Isaiah 64:4 NASB

Our God is like no other. He hears, sees, knows, and understands everything about us. No other power created the entire universe. There has never been another god who was able to create a human, let alone from dirt. None but the one true God hung the sun, moon, or stars in space and set the boundaries of the deep waters. The God of the Bible is the One Who tells the rain when to fall or the wind where to blow. He is the One Who set time in motion and puts it in the hearts of birds when to fly to warmer climates.

And this same God is the One Who acts on behalf of those who wait for Him. An outpouring of His wisdom, an infilling of His power, an overflowing of His grace, or an expression of His love, are but a few of the gifts He has given to those who watch and wait on Him.

In those times when life feels overwhelming, wait on God and praise Him as Paul did in Ephesians 3:20–21, "Now to Him who is able to do far more abundantly beyond all that we ask or think, according to the power that works within us, to Him be the glory in the church and in Christ Jesus to all generations forever and ever. Amen." Take whatever is on your heart to God. Trust Him to show you the answers you need at the time He knows you need them.

For a glimpse of God's creation, listen to and watch "Louie Giglio, Indescribable." Be ready to be amazed and soak in the wonder of our mighty God.

–Susan Sage

QUIET WAITING

It is good that a man should hope and quietly
wait for the salvation of the Lord.
Lamentations 3:26 ESV

Jeremiah went through hard times. For years he preached to the inhabitants of Jerusalem about turning back to God, but they did not bother to listen. Enemies captured Jerusalem and Jeremiah suffered alongside the people of the city. He experienced deep anxiety, which he poured out directly to God. Yet in the middle of the long lamentation in Lamentations 3, his tone changed.

He said, "But this I call to mind, and therefore I have hope" (Lamentations 3:21 ESV). And then Jeremiah had peace. He ended by saying that it is good to wait for God in quietness.

Jeremiah seemed to take on the idea of yet. During affliction, God is faithful. We can also choose to say the same. After every difficulty, God is faithful, and so there is hope.

We have many questions for God. Various pressures draw us in different directions. Sometimes God takes His children into situations where questions fall silent. We learn to wait in quietness and simply put our trust in Him. Job stated that after his trials it was his turn to "lay my hand on my mouth" (Job 40:4 ESV), to be silent before God.

In quietness, we can let go of senseless striving and trust God to be God. We learn that He is different from what we imagined. We cannot define Him, and above all, God has countless possibilities to give us help, even ones that we know nothing about yet. As a matter of fact, in the waiting we learn our secret weapon is "in quietness and in trust shall be your strength" (Isaiah 30:15 ESV).

There is hope yet. The fact that we are still here, asking for help, is an indication that He has sustained our life. Allow His quietness to be your strength today. Rest on Him. Trust in Him. Spend a few minutes in silence before Him, and breathe of His peace.

–Anu Ahonen

— *Notes & Prayers* —

TAKE COURAGE

Wait for the Lord; Be strong and let your heart take courage; Yes, wait on the Lord.
Psalms 27:14 NASB

Have you ever ordered an item you needed but didn't know when it would arrive? Perhaps it had to be back-ordered and the company didn't know when it would be in stock. Day by day you wait, but it doesn't come. Have you felt that way toward God? You have a desperate need but God hasn't fulfilled it yet. You wait and wait. No answer.

Today's verse tells us to wait on the Lord. It also says to be strong and for our hearts to take courage. While we are waiting, we can be strong in our confidence that we will receive an answer in God's timing. Our hearts can have courage because we know God is faithful.

Waiting is not easy. We live in a world of instant gratification. Drive-through restaurants give us a meal or treat within minutes. Our bank account can be accessed in a matter of seconds and shoots out the money we requested. God doesn't tend to work that way. Yes, sometimes He does provide immediately but often we have to wait. The phrase "wait on the Lord" is seen several times in Scripture.

Having to wait goes against our grain. It's hard. When we are searching for clarity, we want to hear from God right away. And He has invited us to come boldly and ask Him for anything we need. But God offers the opportunity for us to learn to trust Him while we wait.

What do you do when you're waiting on God for an answer? Do you wring your hands and fret? Have you tried to just wait and rest knowing God will give you an answer in His time? Which is more profitable?

During the waiting, you can read the Bible to strengthen your faith. As your heart gets stronger, so will your courage. Time spent waiting can be a wonderful way to grow and to know God better.

–Julie Wilson Smith

— *Notes & Prayers* —

MIND GAMES

*For the weapons of our warfare are not of the flesh but have
divine power to destroy strongholds. We destroy arguments
and every lofty opinion raised against the knowledge of God,
and take every thought captive to obey Christ.*
2 Corinthians 10:4–5 ESV

Sometimes medicine helps fight physical pain, and sometimes
it doesn't. Other times, emotional pain outweighs physical pain.
The anxiety of having constant reminders that one's body isn't
playing fair can often be worse than the pain.

What do we do when we've physically done everything possible
to find relief to no avail? How can we manage the emotional toll
physical pain may cause?

Stepping away from the natural to begin fighting where the
real battle is raging—in the spirit—may prove to be the most
effective pill for our souls. As born-again believers, we have the
authority to destroy strongholds. As King's kids, we have the
power to defeat any spiritual onslaught the enemy brings before
us. To properly use our spiritual armament, we need to learn
to bring our emotions into submission to the Spirit by taking
authority over suggestions that the enemy whispers in our minds.
With our minds, we have the power to lift ourselves or tear
ourselves down; to believe or doubt; to become victors or victims.
The choice is ours.

Ask yourself, "What will I embrace, and what will I cast down?"

The next time the enemy starts playing mind games, choose to
become the lifted, believing victor, then repeat these words:

Since my weapons of mass destruction are powerful enough to
destroy strongholds, by the power invested in me by God's Spirit,
I hereby cast down arguments and lofty opinions against me that

have raised themselves against the knowledge of Christ. I now take captive every thought that is not of God. I only welcome thoughts of peace, and not of evil, thoughts that promise me a future and hope, in Jesus's name, amen!

Now, hold on to that victory like the mighty warrior you are!

-Sharon Williams

Notes & Prayers

_____

_____

_____

_____

_____

_____

_____

_____

_____

OUR GOOD SHEPHERD

*I am the good shepherd. The good shepherd lays
down his life for the sheep.*
John 10:11 ESV

The image of the good shepherd with a flock of sheep is a common one, especially in church circles. For those of us who grew up in church, we heard the story of the good shepherd frequently. The sheep knew their shepherd's voice and came when he called. They trusted him completely and followed him wherever he went.

The shepherd knew his sheep and the sheep knew him. The shepherd would protect the sheep from those who would kill and destroy them. If the sheep were in danger, the shepherd would risk his own life to protect the sheep.

Shepherds still tend sheep today. Sadly, these animals are prone to get distracted and wander off. When this happens, the shepherd leaves the flock to seek out and find the lost sheep. He calls the sheep by name and beckons them to come.

This is one of the most common images of Jesus and His heart for us. He is the Good Shepherd and we are the sheep. We, too, tend to get distracted and wander off from the presence of God. Because of His great love for us, our Good Shepherd, Jesus, will always come looking for us and guide us back. If we are hurt, He will carry us home.

Our Good Shepherd paid the ultimate price to save us when He died on the cross to pay the price for our sins. Jesus laid down His life so we may live life abundantly. There is no greater love than this.

Take a few moments to imagine yourself as a sheep curling up to sleep in the green grasses next to your Good Shepherd. Look into His loving face and see Him smiling down at you. Carry this image with you today.

–Jodine Zeitler

Notes & Prayers

_____

_____

_____

_____

_____

_____

_____

_____

_____

_____

O WORSHIP THE KING

Far above all rule and authority and power and dominion,
and above every name that is named, not only in this age
but also in the one to come.
Ephesians 1:21 esv

Do you ever have days when you feel Satan is winning? Does it seem like the powers of the world are overtaking and you're powerless to win in your illness battles?

The Lord reminds us that His power is perfected in our weakness and that His grace is sufficient for anything a day brings (2 Corinthians 12:9).

But when pain screams, we need to consider firm truths about the scope of God's power. It is important to remember that our all-powerful King is fully reigning over our pain, within the entire universe He created. We can sing great hymns and songs to remind us that His power is "far above all."

"O worship the King, All glorious above, O gratefully sing His power and His love: Our shield and defender, the Ancient of Days, pavilioned in splendor, And girded with praise!" Jesus is our King! ("O Worship the King," Grant, R., 1833). The resurrection really happened; Jesus is enthroned above fulfilling His kingdom purposes right now. And this was all predicted in prophecy millennia ago.

Satan is not winning. On the cross, Jesus "disarmed the rulers and authorities and put them to open shame, by triumphing over them in him" (Colossians 2:15 esv). Jesus already won, which means Jesus's triumph is also ours. No matter how severe the pain of Satan's attack, we are forever upheld by our all-powerful King Who has good Kingdom purposes. Even in pain. Let us continue to sing, enduring pain with trust in our Savior-King.

"Frail children of dust, and feeble as frail, in you do we trust, nor find you to fail. Your mercies, how tender, how firm to the end, our Maker, Defender, Redeemer, and Friend!" ("O Worship the King," Grant, R.,1833).

What song might you sing to help you remember His power and His love for you today? Sing to your King.

-Lauri Hogle

———— *Notes & Prayers* ————

OUR TRUE GIFTS

Each one must give as he has decided in his heart,
not reluctantly or under compulsion,
for God loves a cheerful giver.
2 Corinthians 9:7 ESV

Black Friday draws a lot of attention in our country. It is heavily advertised as the most advantageous day to get the best discounts and deals on merchandise. Some of us never physically enter a brick-and-mortar store, choosing rather to peruse various internet sites, complete with notifications and price alerts. Others prefer the hands-on method, touring one place of business after another. It's a big event!

Media pressure is so unrelenting that many conglomerates have succumbed to a Black Friday expansion stretched to include several days before and after Thanksgiving. It is a cultural announcement saying, "Christmas is just around the corner! Think gifts, gifts, gifts!"

As believers, we can step away from the hype and give from a better perspective than society might otherwise dictate. The origin of real gifts cannot be found on any shelf. Nor is it only available on Gray Thursdays or Black Fridays. A believer's gifts are found nestled within the heart through the messages and instructions received from the Holy Spirit. The joy to be found within these gifts is that they are available to us 365 days each year.

Not every gift is readily recognized. Some can be cloaked inside a kind soul who loves and prays faithfully from afar. Others can be the listening ear that has heard the same story told over and over but still responds with an authentic measure of interest as if it's being heard for the first time. It can be the quiet completion of a task for another when it's long past bedtime.

We should never underestimate either giving or receiving these true gifts from a willing spirit. They are pure and intentional, but most importantly, full of love!

What true gifts (and to whom) do you have waiting in your spirit to be delivered?

–Melanie Stiles

Notes & Prayers

Notes & Prayers

WHO DO OTHERS SEE?

He must increase, but I must decrease.
John 3:30 NASB

Hebrews 11 is full of spiritual heroes who stepped into their world as normal human beings but then grew into extraordinary examples for us. If we take time to read about them, we will find individuals who made mistakes, chose the wrong path for a time, set their eyes on the wrong goal, but eventually made the right life-changing decision.

Rahab, although known as a harlot, made a choice of faith resulting in the rescue of her and her family (Joshua 2). Gideon was scared and hid in a winepress but stepped into how God saw him and lead his people to victory with only a few warriors (Judges 6–8). Ruth left her home and culture and eventually found herself in the family line of Christ (The book of Ruth and Matthew 1).

These people became involved in a process as they learned to trust God through life's difficulties. They may have still made mistakes, but the transformation happened because they chose to allow the work God was doing in their hearts to match their actions and attitudes.

When we choose to live mindful of God, aware of His gifts and presence, and focused on His purposes, we may realize life is for His glory and for walking in deep connection with Him. And we desire to live out the truth of John 3:30.

We can choose to exist for ourselves, always striving to get ahead and gaining all the possessions we can. The result will be emptiness because something will always be missing.

Because we were created for a relationship with God, nothing else will fill the part of us reserved solely for Him. By seeking God and all He has for us, we can continue growing in Him each day and allowing Him to become more visible so we can point others to Him.

Is there an area where you need to decrease and let God increase? Where could you ask God to help you seek Him more through a challenging circumstance?

-Susan Sage

Notes & Prayers

FINDING HOPE IN THE SILENCE

My soul, wait in silence for God only.
For my hope is from Him.
Psalms 62:5 NASB

Living with a chronic illness can be difficult in many ways. Sometimes it's hard to figure out a diagnosis for our symptoms. There are well-meaning friends and family members who may say, "When I had that symptom, I took this and it really helped me." Another person may say, "Well, that didn't work for me." Even doctors may disagree regarding the diagnosis and treatment. You may feel you have a lot of voices in your head shouting advice. You might want to throw your hands up in the air and scream, "What am I supposed to do? Who should I listen to?"

When Jesus was on earth, multitudes of people often cried out to Him for healing or for other requests. He frequently left His trusted disciples to seek out a place where He could be alone to talk with God. If Jesus needed to get away from the noise, how much more do we?

Sometimes we need to find a place to be still and quiet. We don't need a cacophony of voices. We only need God's, and we often hear Him best when we are silent and alone.

The last part of today's verse tells us where we can find hope. It isn't the type of hope a friend might say, such as, "I hope you feel better." But rather, this hope is a deep, calm assurance God gives us. It comes from knowing He has everything under control and we don't need to worry. All other voices are quieted when we place our hope in Him.

What noise is causing you distress? Are there too many tasks you're trying to accomplish? Are there too many voices clamoring for your attention?

Do you have a special place you like to go to find quiet and peace? Get away with God in prayer. He will give your heart and mind peace.

–Julie Wilson Smith

Notes & Prayers

_____

_____

_____

_____

_____

_____

_____

_____

Notes & Prayers

JUST BREATHE

He breathed on them . . .
John 20:22a ESV

God created and molded man. Though man was there, he was nothing more than a statue or a mannequin. Yet, once God breathed into him, man became a living, thinking, breathing soul.

Now, fast forward to Jesus's crucifixion. When He died, His disciples had no idea what their future held. Their Savior, whom they trusted with their lives, was gone, and thoughts of what would become of them likely bombarded the disciples' minds. Then, after Jesus resurrected, He appeared to them, and showed them His wounds. Jesus then spoke peace over them, commissioned them, and breathed on them. While the disciples thrilled at seeing their Messiah, they still had no idea what to expect next. Yet the simple act of receiving Jesus's breath before His departure was an assurance that no matter what they would face, they could continue to breathe because of Him.

Sometimes life's situations can cause us to hold our breath in shock, dismay, or anticipation. But we can't sustain our lives with bated breath. One must breathe to live.

Whether you feel like holding on or letting go, remember to breathe. As you begin to feel secure in the Master's hand, inhale the breath of His Spirit, and exhale the frustrations you've been bottling up. Inhale the truth of God's promises and exhale the toxins of your doubt. Inhale the goodness of God's Word and exhale the lies that have kept you bound.In your breath, there is life. The wind of God's Spirit is breathing a fresh breath on you so you can breathe again. So, just breathe.

–Sharon Williams

Notes & Prayers

NEVER BEYOND THE PRIZE

Every athlete exercises self-control in all things. They do it to receive a perishable wreath, but we an imperishable. So I do not run aimlessly; I do not box as one beating the air.
1 Corinthians 9:25–26 ESV

Every couple of years, the world focuses on the Olympics, which showcases the best athletes each nation has to offer. We watch with awe and respect, considering the training and self-discipline it took each athlete to achieve the level of skill and competence necessary to compete.

Similarly, in biblical times, the highly competitive Corinthian society hosted an event similar to the Olympics where athletes would compete to win honor, and a wreath was placed on their heads like a crown. However, this wreath would soon wither and die, and the honor they achieved would fade with time.

The apostle Paul compared the training and self-control of a highly trained athlete with the self-discipline and self-denial he chose to live by as he served the Lord and others. To win as many as possible to the faith, the prize Paul sought was an unfading, heavenly one. This prize was along with the salvation Jesus freely gave that could never be earned. Paul lived his life with a definite purpose. His self-disciplined focus showed this.

With chronic pain and conditions, we may often feel that the thrill of any type of prize is beyond our capabilities. However, Paul showed us a different way to live: to run a good race with an eternal goal in mind, to spread the good news of salvation through Jesus to as many people as possible, and to receive a heavenly prize.

Just like an Olympian, we can train ourselves with self-discipline in our spiritual lives including things such as prayer,

Bible reading, and fellowship with other believers. We can then allow the Holy Spirit to strengthen us to share with others and guide us to those who need to hear about Jesus and be saved.

How can you train yourself with self-discipline in your spiritual life today?

–Jodine Zeitler

—— Notes & Prayers ——

SET YOUR MINDS ON THINGS THAT ARE ABOVE

Set your minds on things that are above,
not things that are on earth.
Colossians 3:2 ESV

Many days, our minds are naturally filled with earthly things, keeping our body's needs at bay, our to-do lists, plans, and people. But when symptoms hit hard, we then enter thought battles. "If I can't do these things, what good am I?" "Who am I?" God tells us how to win. He helps us to reset our minds on things above, things of our transformed life and identity in Christ (Colossians 3:3).

Let's arm up for battle when our thoughts and emotions flood. He transforms and renovates our thoughts, feelings, desires, and purposes (Romans 12:2) as we seek Him from the sickbed. How? By His Word. God's speaking through Scripture provides His comfort, encouragement, conviction, and desires for a life of illness. As we surrender this earthly life and our desires, what is He saying to our thoughts today? Is He teaching us to give thanks (Colossians 3:17) as we endure symptoms? Could we praise our Savior and Redeemer, our Suffering Servant who intimately empathizes with our pain (Hebrews 4:14–16)? Is He reminding us to rest in His unchanging character, presence, and work as we suffer? Is He reminding us of who we are, in Christ (Ephesians 1)?

Because He's living in us through His Spirit (1 Corinthians 6:19–20; Titus 3:5; 2 Peter 1:4), He's with us in the sickbed. He's helping us reset our minds, to understand Scripture (1 Corinthians 2:12), empowering us to live for Jesus to do His will (Galatians 5:16) and produce fruit (Galatians 5:22–23). Even on the sickbed. In Christ, this becomes our song:

"Praise, my soul, the King of heaven; to his feet your tribute bring. Ransomed, healed, restored, forgiven, evermore his praises sing. Alleluia, alleluia! Praise the everlasting King!" ("Praise My Soul, the King of Heaven!," Lyte, H. F., 1834).

What Scriptures remind you of who you are in Christ? Will you read, listen to, and study Scripture today, to set your mind on things above?

–Lauri Hogle

Notes & Prayers

_____

_____

_____

_____

_____

_____

_____

_____

_____

OUR GOOD REPORTS

They shall pour forth the fame of your abundant goodness
and shall sing aloud of your righteousness.
Psalm 145:7 ESV

Traditionally, when we hear someone has received a "good report," our minds likely assume a positive medical prognosis is coming. It is a representation of our current culture. Yet as we meditate on the biblical rendition of the words, it becomes evident there is no physical aspect included. A "good report" could be declared at any time by any one of us. The Bible states a good report is defined as whatever is good. It is composed of one sound bit of truth or wisdom that stirs the heart enough to rejoice.

Declaring a good report is a proactive decision. We have taken on the option of searching out what is going right in our world. It requires us to recognize what we are grateful for and what holds value, often despite what might be less than perfect. It takes eyes of faith and determination that are willing to identify what, at first, may not be the thing most prevalent in our minds. Many blessings can be hidden underneath the noises of life.

There may be more than a few days when we are tempted to believe the only good report available to us simply must come out of the medical field, but we are composed of so much more than our fleshly failings or successes.

We have a spiritual body that can always find a reason to celebrate. The act of taking hold of even one singular promise from God or even inhaling the fragrance of one rose has the power to spark a flame that can spread throughout our countenance. It can then travel outward to become a breath of fresh spiritual air to others.

In the end, this is not only beneficial to our bodily health but also creates an opportunity for our joy in the Lord to influence others.

Have you given thought to what your good report could be for today? Are you prepared to share it?

–Melanie Stiles

Notes & Prayers

_____

_____

_____

_____

_____

_____

_____

_____

_____

GOD WILL RESTORE

O Lord, you have brought up my soul from Sheol;
you restored me to life from among
those who go down to the pit.
Psalm 30:3 ESV

How we long to be strengthened and restored! In Psalm 30:3, David exclaimed that God had restored him to strength. Throughout his life, he had been tested in many ways. He found himself in extreme circumstances with no options. The dangerous situations had lasted so long and been so stressful that we can only wonder how he coped. Many times, he had been in danger of his life, and he was eventually even persecuted by a family member.

Also, in the above psalm, there was a situation where David had possibly been seriously ill. All his vitality had already waned. But he knew where his help came from. He turned to God, and God raised him and made him alive and well again.

David did not get stuck in the heavy issues, instead, he gave thanks to God (Psalm 30:4). This psalm of praise was written for the occasion of celebrating the site of the future temple. In it, David directed his praise straight to God and recognized what God had done for him. He had a close and personal relationship with God and focused his attention on Him often.

David was both a warlike king and a poet. In the psalms, he used imagery from his own life. Many times, he fled from his pursuers into the shelter provided by the mountains. So, he called God his stronghold, a safe refuge (2 Samuel 22:3).

As David did, we can also lift our eyes straight to God. If the waves of life are raging high and we have ended up in deep waters, He can save and restore us.

In difficult times, God is a safe and secure stronghold. We would do well to follow David's example of praising and crying out to God.

Make a list of ways God has responded to your prayers in the past. Keep it close by as a reminder of His care.

–Anu Ahonen

— Notes & Prayers —

BLESSING GOD

To Him who sits on the throne, and to the Lamb,
be blessing and honor and glory and
dominion forever and ever.
Revelation 5:13 NASB

Have you ever sought, wished for, or asked for God's blessing? Maybe you have hoped for a blessing given by someone you love. A blessing from God would include His favor, mercy, a gift, or something else not currently possessed. From another person, it might be approval or good wishes.

But how often do we think about blessing God? This can happen when our hearts are in tune with Who He is and all He's done and then praise Him for Who He is. Throughout Scripture, we can find many instances of praise given to God. Writers of the psalms penned many of their songs and pleas with this theme. Worship preceded prayers of forgiveness from men like Daniel, Ezekiel, and Isaiah.

The book of Revelation is filled with examples of blessings for God. "Worthy are You to take the book and to break its seals" (Revelation 5:9). "Worthy is the Lamb that was slain to receive power and riches and wisdom and might and honor and glory and blessing" (Revelation 5:12). "Great and marvelous are Your works, O Lord God, the Almighty; Righteous and true are Your ways, King of the nations" (Revelation 15:3).

If you're not sure where to begin, Psalm 106:1 is a beautiful place to start by blessing Him: "Praise the LORD! Oh give thanks to the LORD, for He is good; For His lovingkindness is everlasting."

When life is full of challenges; when illness is at the height of a cycle; when discouragement threatens, by directing thoughts and whispering words of blessing to God, the mood of the blesser can lift as a connection is made with God.

Take a few moments today and focus on God's character. Thank Him for Who He is and for all He means personally. Bless God and be blessed.

–Susan Sage

JESUS IS STILL STANDING

But he, full of the Holy Spirit, gazed into heaven and saw
the glory of God, and Jesus standing at the right hand of God.
And he said, "Behold, I see the heavens opened,
and the Son of Man standing at the right hand of God."
Acts 7:55–56 ESV

Have you ever noticed how far some people go to protect their siblings as children? When someone would hear a sibling was being bullied, he or she would arrive on the scene and stand by, ready to take the bully on alone if necessary. Jesus may have felt like that protective sibling, prepared to stand in front of Stephen and conquer the bullies. But, while He didn't stop the fight, He did stand up!

Jesus knew full well that the ultimate victory over the disciple-killers would require Him to stand up and go toe-to-toe with this adversary strategically. He did and stood to receive the sacrifice that was Stephen.

We need to stop and reflect on the tragic or trying events we've overcome and how we've been delivered. Now, picture Jesus standing up. We may have battle scars remaining from physical, mental, or spiritual wars we've engaged in, yet healing is ours because He stood up. As He stood up for Stephen, trust that He's standing up for you.

Acknowledging that Jesus is standing for you, take a moment to utter this prayer of thanksgiving: Thank You because You stood in the gap and wrapped Yourself in flesh to feel my infirmities. Thank You because You stood to hang on the cross to redeem my sins. Thank You for standing on my behalf and freeing the captives from captivity and becoming the great gift Giver (Ephesians 4:8). Thank You because You stood on the third day as my resurrected

Lord, my head, and made me a part of Your glorious Body. Thank You, Jesus, because when the devil stood up, so did You! Thank You, Lord, for yet standing for me.

Today, thank Jesus for the places He has stood for you.

–Sharon Williams

———— *Notes & Prayers* ————

LET YOUR LOVE SHINE

Let all that you do be done in love.
1 Corinthians 16:14 NASB

Love is one of the most widely used words in the English language. To express affection, we say, "I love you." To express approval, we say, "I love your outfit" or another platitude. We have feelings of love in varying degrees for those we hold dear. These are all valid applications of the word "love," though not necessarily the best. Looking at 1 Corinthians 16:14, we see we are to let all we do be done in love. This implies love as an action or a way of doing things. But how do we go about letting all we do be done lovingly? That is a tall order.

Before we can even try to do everything in love, we must understand what is being asked of us. Just a few chapters before, in 1 Corinthians 13, we read what love truly is: "Love is patient and kind; love does not envy or boast; it is not arrogant or rude. It does not insist on its own way; it is not irritable or resentful; it does not rejoice at wrongdoing, but rejoices with the truth. Love bears all things, believes all things, hopes all things, endures all things. Love never ends" (vv. 4–8a ESV). If we need an example of what love looks like, we can see, through the life of Jesus, what it means to truly do everything in love.

To do this takes an intentional, conscious effort. It won't just happen, and we can't do it on our own. In prayer we receive guidance from the Holy Spirit within us to show us how Jesus would be loving in everyday circumstances. When we act out of God's love, we shine the light of Jesus to everyone around us. As you go through your day, intentionally look for ways you can do all things in love. Ask the Spirit for guidance to help you see how to do as Jesus did.

–Jodine Zeitler

LOOKING TO OUR POWERFUL HELPER

I lift up my eyes to the hills. From where does my help come?
Psalm 121:1 ESV

God gave us a journey of climbing hills. As with His people singing Psalm 121, one of the Song of Ascents, we sometimes climb into darkness. We walk through mountainous dangers, desert heat, and torrential storms. Sometimes the vistas are wide and breath-taking. Other times, narrow cliffs feel precarious and our enemy lurks as a robber to steal our joy, peace, and hope.

Psalm 121 instructs us to look up to our Helper while on a difficult journey. Hebrews exhorts us: "Let us then with confidence draw near to the throne of grace, that we may receive mercy and find grace to help in time of need" (Hebrews 4:16 ESV).

Who is our Helper? He's the One Who, in His supreme power and reigning authority, created the hills.

"I sing th'almighty power of God that made the mountains rise, that spread the flowing seas abroad and built the lofty skies, I sing the wisdom that ordained the sun to rule the day; the moon shines full at his command and all the stars obey" ("I Sing th'almighty Power of God," Watts, I., 1715).

Our Helper is the power-full One Who drew us to Himself through faith in Jesus Christ, by grace (John 6:44, 65). The Holy Spirit, our Helper, dwells within us (John 14:26). He who sits on the throne is continually available to provide His compassionate help to us as we climb each day's mountain.

"May the God of hope fill you with all joy and peace in believing, so that by the power of the Holy Spirit you may abound in hope." (Romans 15:13 ESV)

As we climb along the challenging journey, His power and His presence are with us. Let's lift our eyes to our Helper, believe the Word of God, and ask Him to continually fill us with His joy, peace, and hope as we ascend the hills of our illness journey.

-Lauri Hogle

Notes & Prayers

YOUR OPEN DOOR

I know your works. Behold, I have set before you
an open door, which no one is able to shut. I know
that you have but little power, and yet you have
kept my word and have not denied my name.
Revelation 3:8 ESV

Today's verse defines how the Lord felt about the church at Philadelphia and its works. From what is said, we can see how obeying the Word and staying loyal to Jesus is very important. This church had a secular calling which caused it to maintain an open door to nonbelievers seeking to know Jesus. Later in the passage, Jesus is so impressed with their successes that He promised to keep the church from the tribulation period. Can you think of a more wonderful promise?

We can, hopefully, agree that the open door of the church represents the open hearts of the congregation as well. As we know, any church is comprised of those persons who inhabit it. In our current culture, open hearts are becoming few and far between. To interact with others who believe differently than we do can be a tall order. Yet it is what Jesus chose to honor.

Listening to others with an open heart does not mean we have to agree with someone's viewpoints. It is simply an action that shows we respect them as fellow children of God. In the end, it's up to Him, not us, to sort out our journeys independently.

Under any circumstances, a quiet, calm interchange could surely accomplish far more than loud outbursts or insinuations of supreme doctrine. Imagine those who walked through the open door of the church in Philadelphia and the ensuing conversations afterward. We can't realistically believe those talks were not full of controversial "other gods," and there must have been sizable conversions despite their differences. It would be prudent to ask ourselves how the open hearts of those who greeted them made a difference. It would also be wise to follow their example.

What does "open-hearted" mean to you? How can you practice this behavior?

–Melanie Stiles

Notes & Prayers

_____

_____

_____

_____

_____

_____

_____

_____

WHY JESUS WEPT

Jesus wept.
John 11:35 ESV

Three times in the New Testament, Jesus's crying is mentioned (John 11:35; Luke 19:41; Hebrews 5:7–9) What was it that made Jesus cry? He was moved when people had to face the death of a loved one. He also mourned for the people of Jerusalem, their lack of understanding, and finally, because of what He would face in the final hours of His life, He cried as He called out to His Father.

In the Old Testament, we read of the prophet Isaiah describing Jesus (Isaiah 53:3–5). Isaiah prophesied that Jesus would be a Man of sorrows and familiar with pain. Outwardly, Jesus would look so broken by suffering that people would turn away so they wouldn't have to look at Him.

Mankind was created for paradise but ended up being expelled from the beautiful garden to a harsher environment. Outside of what God planned, people started to rebel and hate each other and God. Jesus came into the midst of this brokenness.

Much of Scripture is almost like God's prolonged lament for humankind. After the humans He'd created rejected Him, He had to stoop down to humanity to redeem it. He sacrificed what was most precious to Him. His own Son.

As God left Jesus on the cross as the sacrifice for mankind, Jesus released the most painful wail of all: "My God, my God, why have you forsaken me?" (Matthew 27:46 ESV). His cry crystallized the entire pain and loneliness of mankind.

Because of what Jesus did on the cross, and because He then defeated death by rising from the dead, redemption was made complete. The relationship between God and His creation was restored.

When sorrow is heavy and pain is wearying, remember God understands. He hears and sees when we cry. And He grieves for the pain we find ourselves in.

Thank Him for caring enough to redeem your relationship with Him. Lean on His strength to help you through the struggles. Let Him ease your tears.

–Anu Ahonen

--- Notes & Prayers ---

LOVE ONE ANOTHER

Beloved, let us love one another, for love is from God;
and everyone who loves is born of God and knows God.
1 John 4:7 NASB

The years of coronavirus were unusual ones, to say the least. Most of us had never seen anything like it. Churches, schools, and restaurants were closed. We were told to stay home for our protection. Visiting family and friends was frowned upon. These precautions caused many people to feel isolated.

But for those of us who live with chronic illness, we are all too familiar with this feeling. Often, we don't feel well enough to go places. We can begin to feel alone; especially if friends and family don't call or come by to check on us.

It is important for each of us to feel loved and cared for. We know God loves us, but we also need the human touch. What if, on those days of not feeling well, we purposefully changed our thinking?

Even if we don't feel well, we can show love to others. Sending a card with a short note in it doesn't take much effort at all. On days when we feel better, we can call and check on a friend or family member. Think how much that would mean to show this kind of love to others.

When we get our focus off of ourselves and onto others, we feel better. We receive a blessing by demonstrating concern for our circle of family and friends.

Love is from God. If we love God, then we are to love others. By loving others, we demonstrate God's love toward them by letting them know we care.

Do you have special ways to reach out to others? Cards? Phone calls? Perhaps you enjoy making cookies for a friend or neighbor? Find your unique way of reaching out and see how it encourages others.

–Julie Wilson Smith

— *Notes & Prayers* —

TODAY

For I consider that the sufferings of this present
time are not worthy to be compared with the glory
That is to be revealed to us.
Romans 8:18 NASB

Do you ever feel like there's no hope for chronic issues? Aches and illness can feel like they will last forever. No matter what anyone tells us, sometimes we become fearful that tomorrow will not be different.

But what if we focused only on today? Matthew 6:27 says, "And who of you by being worried can add a single hour to his life?" Worry can bring more stress causing unnecessary exhaustion and weakness.

Can you imagine if we could gain time by worrying? People might live longer, but would life be better? Of course not, because there's nothing positive or beneficial about agonizing over things. How can we keep from drowning in hopelessness or allowing negative thoughts to pull us lower?

Matthew 6:34 encourages us to focus on today and not tomorrow. Romans 8 guides us to think about all God has for us as we live in a relationship with Him.

Paul gives the best advice in Philippians 4 when he lists what we should think about. He reminds us to guard our hearts and minds so God's peace can prevail. He also tells us to think about truth, honor, righteousness, purity, loveliness, excellence, and everything worthy of God's praise. That's quite a list.

Instead of being overwhelmed by what might or might not happen, let's redirect our attention.

What are you able to do today? Are you able to get up and

shower? Praise God. Can you make yourself a cup of coffee or make your child's lunch? Praise God. Would you be able to text a friend to tell them you're thinking about them? Praise God. Can you see? Thank God for your sight. Take a breath. Thank Him you can breathe.

Focus on what you can do right now. Exchange hopelessness for God's eternal hope. Thank Him for today. Contemplate Psalm 118:24. Rejoice in what you have right now. Leave tomorrow to God.

–Susan Sage

———— *Notes & Prayers* ————

STRENGTH FOR TODAY

Finally, be strong in the Lord and in
the strength of His might.
Ephesians 6:10 ESV

In our world, strength is widely sought after. Many people exercise to keep their bodies strong. Others read and study to keep their minds sharp. And others turn to business to make their financial portfolios resilient. These are all ways people seek to be strong by their might.

There is a common feeling that with strength comes power. For those of us with chronic pain and conditions, feeling strong can be a rare and elusive sensation. As believers, thankfully, we serve a Mighty God Who desires to strengthen us from His power and might.

Throughout the Bible, God is referred to as Almighty God. The Hebrew name for "mighty God" is El Gibbor. "El" meaning "the one true God," and "Gibbor" meaning "strong and mighty." Before Jesus was even born, His name was called Mighty God. There are many verses in the Bible referring to God as mighty and giving evidence of His strength, power, and might.

As we read the Gospels, we see He has miraculously proven His power over nature, disease, demons, sin, and death. Yet He doesn't hoard His divine strength. He chooses to empower us with it.

Jesus sent the Holy Spirit to enable us to go into the world and proclaim His love to others. Through His power, we can shine His light in a world impacted by sin. He gives us the strength to face each new day and whatever may come with it. But we must choose to accept this gift and live in it.

If we turn our backs on God's offer of strength and choose to continue under our power, He won't force Himself on us. If we ever feel a lack of strength, we may be pulling from our power, not the Lord's. Because He is all-powerful, His strength will never fail.

Where do you need to turn to the Lord and accept His offer of strength today?

–Jodine Zeitler

Notes & Prayers

WHO AM I?

I have been crucified with Christ. It is no longer
I who live, but Christ who lives in me.
And the life I now live in the flesh I live by faith in
the Son of God, who loved me, and gave himself for me.
Gal. 2:20 ESV

For those with chronic health issues, questions may plague us like, Who am I? Am I a "sick person"? Is "chronic illness sufferer" my identity? Is my label "chronic illness warrior"?

Do you resonate with the sick man by the pool in John 5? Along with huge crowds of chronically ill people, he'd been ailing and disabled for thirty-eight years. Jesus knew this and chose him, out of multitudes, asking, "Do you want to be healed?" (John 5:6 ESV). The answer would change everything for and about the man.

In the same way He asked the man if he wanted to be healed, Jesus asks us, "Do you want your identity to be healed? Do you want your sin to be healed by My stripes? Do you want permanent hope, for all eternity? Do you want to be Mine, crucified, unified with Me? Are you willing to experience any pain or suffering life might bring, in this fallen world, while knowing you are with Me now and will be with Me forever?"

Immanuel knows our names. God says, "Fear not, for I have redeemed you; I have called you by name, you are mine" (Isaiah 43:1ESV). Jesus Christ who lives in us has sealed us by His indwelling Spirit (Ephesians 4:30).

We have taken His name, as His bride, as believers. Redeemed by His blood, our bodies are sick...but we are still His. In our ill bodies, He is our actual life and identity.

So, we sing and remember who we are and Whose we are: "My hope is built on nothing less than Jesus's blood and righteousness" ("My Hope Is Built on Nothing Less," Mote, E., 1834).

In whatever you are dealing with, how can you rest in your true identity?

-Lauri Hogle

Notes & Prayers

WHAT REALLY MATTERS

But let your adorning be the hidden person of the heart
with the imperishable beauty of a gentle and quiet spirit,
which in God's sight is very precious.
1 Peter 3:4 ESV

Perhaps you remember the way our mothers and grandmothers liberally applied what they called cold creams to every pore on their faces faithfully. Little did we realize that we would soon follow in their footsteps. It was to be a journey, moving from moisturizers all the way to wrinkle removers.

Our grandmothers were susceptible to never-ending offers of extending their beauty. Through the supposed miracles of cosmetic technology, we have carried the baton forward to the next generations. Yet how many of us have succeeded in finding victory within the crow's feet war?

While we juggle family, careers, community, and self-care, it's interesting how our priorities always seem to be ebbing and flowing. What's important one day is not as important as something else the next day. It can be difficult at the end of a week to sort out what mattered at all. Thank goodness we have a God Who doesn't place values as we tend to do.

Our Lord is interested in one primary thing. He is focused on the conditions of our spirits. There is an excellent reason for this. He knows our everlasting beauty flows from there! True beauty resides in each of us as we get to know Jesus more and more. It radiates through our love walk and our spiritual nature.

No cream can ever provide ingredients that will match what God has already placed within us. All we have to do is remember where to look.

God knows what we look like, both inside and out. He knows what to provide, beyond any physical manifestation, to align our spirits with Him and His purposes.

Ask Him to show you the beauty He sees in you today.

–Melanie Stiles

Notes & Prayers

WISDOM

But the wisdom from above is first pure,
then peaceable, gentle, Reasonable, full of mercy and
good fruits, unwavering, without hypocrisy.
James 3:17 NASB

Have you ever pondered the Old Testament patriarch Abraham's journey from Ur of the Chaldeans to the land of Canaan? God had called him to start toward the unknown land of promise. There must have been many problems associated with moving the whole company and all the animals. It was not at all clear how they would reach their destination.

The New Testament tells us that Abraham did not know where he was going (Hebrews 11:8). He had to learn to trust God's guidance without knowing or seeing beforehand. It is this that makes him an example of faith. How could Abraham know how to solve the problems they faced so that in the end they would reach the right place?

When Abraham and his nephew Lot's herds had grown large, they had to separate. Without this parting, there would not be enough pastureland for all their animals. How could the situation be resolved?

Abraham allowed his nephew Lot to choose the land he wanted, and Lot chose the verdant, well-watered Jordan plain. Abraham simply went in the opposite direction. Only later did God confirm his decision as correct.

What could we learn from all this? First, God sees the Christian's daily walk and is interested in his everyday life. Second, He knows circumstances can be complex and they may demand a new kind of orientation. He can use every detail in life to guide His children.

If we have come to a turning point in life and cannot see the road ahead, we need wisdom from above to move forward in faith and trust. Where do you need wisdom today? Ask God for His perspective, and trust Him to lead in the way He knows is best.

–Anu Ahonen

———— *Notes & Prayers* ————

PERFECT PEACE

The steadfast of mind You will keep in perfect peace,
because he trusts in You.
Isaiah 26:3 NASB

When illness flares up our minds can quickly become consumed with thoughts of how we feel. "This hurts." "I'm so tired." On and on like a continuous reel.

Does that ever happen to you? Do you feel so miserable all you can concentrate on is how you're feeling at the moment? It's not very productive, is it? But we can have a peaceful mind amid our suffering. Better yet, we can have a mind and soul that is in perfect peace.

Steadfast means unwavering or fixed. If we change our thoughts and fix them on God, we can begin to experience peace. When our mind wants to wander back to negativity, we need to be unwavering and keep our focus fixed on God. We can consciously change what we're thinking about.

One way we can do this is to train our minds to be thankful for God's blessings. A good tool for this is to make a list. Write down as many specific people and items you can think of that you're grateful for. As you make your list, thank God for each one. You may begin to come up with additional blessings to add. We can choose for our minds to dwell on how badly we feel or we can choose to be thankful. The choice is always ours. By training our thoughts we can learn to cultivate a life that's filled with deep inner peace and contentment.

As we focus on God's goodness toward us our trust in Him deepens. We realize we can depend on Him. There's no need for us to worry because He has promised to take care of us. The deeper our trust in God, the more at peace we become.

How about you? What are you focusing on? Are you thinking about what you are unable to do or are you looking at all the ways God has provided for you? Try making a list of God's blessings.

–Julie Wilson Smith

Notes & Prayers

OUR MASTER THE MAESTRO

There was reclining on Jesus' bosom one of
His disciples, whom Jesus loved.
John 13:23 NASB

When we rest in Jesus, we can get close enough to hear His heartbeat and catch His rhythm. When we catch His rhythm, we become in tune with Him like a piano in tune with its maestro. To hear and feel His heartbeat is to connect with Him and flow in His will.

Due to humidity or changes in temperature, or even relocation, piano strings can loosen causing the piano to go out of tune. Likewise, the strings of our intimacy with God sometimes loosen, causing our lifestyles of worship and spiritual ears to become dull and flat. We no longer have an ear to hear His heartbeat at these times.

Just as varying factors can cause a piano to go out of tune, likewise, there are many conditions we face as Christians that causes us to become flat in our faith and out of tune with our Master creating the need to be re-tuned. Our goal should be to go back to our Tuner and allow Him to retune us to bring us back into alignment with His will. His will is the song of our worship. He is the Master and Maestro of our praise.

When the piano is tuned, the strings are pulled tighter and tighter together until the Master achieves the right pitch and tone. If those strings could talk, they might complain that it is a painful process.

Yet when we allow ourselves to go through the painful process of having our faith pulled and stretched tighter, we ultimately develop the patience necessary to become synchronized with and in tune with Him. Our lives can then begin to make a melody with Him as we fall into harmony with His will (James 1:3–4).

Do you feel that your faith has weakened? Has your worship become stagnant? Take this moment to allow our Master to retune you as you lay in His bosom in worship to make a melody fit for your Lover.

-Sharon Williams

———— *Notes & Prayers* ————

WHAT WE UNDERSTAND

*Beloved, now we are children of God, and it has
not appeared as yet what we will be.
We know that when He appears, we will be like Him,
because we will see Him just as He is.*
1 John 3:2 NASB

Have you ever heard someone introduce themselves by saying their name and what they do before sharing more information?

"Hello, I'm George, and I am a dentist." "Hi, I'm Bridgett, and I am a florist." "Hey, I'm Madison, and I am a lawyer." Too often a person's identity is wrapped up in what they do.

Most likely, even more than with healthy people, we who live with chronic illness and pain have a better understanding that our identity does not come from what we do. Too many days, we may find our ability to do anything is under attack. We understand doing is not equal to who we are.

Unfortunately, at other times, we are tempted to believe our identity is somehow intertwined with a diagnosis or prognosis. It is important to remember the ailment we live with is not who we are.

If we have decided to accept God's gift of forgiveness through the work of Jesus on the cross, we are His children. Period. That is who we are. We are in His family. We are His.

Especially in the middle of pain or illness, if we can focus on these truths, perhaps we will be able to keep from becoming discouraged with what we don't seem to be able to do at the moment. But even when the cycle passes or lessens, we would be wise to remember the same truth.

Once we are God's child, we remain His. In illness. In health. In pain. In strength. According to Romans 8:38–39, circumstances do not change who we are when our identity rests with Christ.

The next time you're feeling less than or unsure of who you are, read the verses shared today. Rest and trust what God says. You are not a label. You are His.

-Susan Sage

Notes & Prayers

THORN IN THE FLESH

So to keep me from becoming conceited because of the surpassing greatness of the revelations, a thorn was given me in the flesh, a messenger of Satan to harass me, to keep me from becoming conceited. Three times I pleaded with the Lord about this, that it should leave me.
2 Corinthians 12:7–8 ESV

We don't know the exact thorn Paul endured, but we know it was painful. It harassed him, nagged him, bothered him. The original word describes something more like a tent stake, not a tiny rose thorn.

So many people think thorns of illness and pain could never be part of the life of a believer. According to Scripture, that's a lie. We know it was given to Paul. He begged God to remove this thorn, repeatedly.

It's not surprising because Paul was actively sharing the gospel, in a life of active ministry. His suffering must have made the work even more challenging.

Our chronic, lingering illnesses not only bring physical suffering but emotional and spiritual ones. Like Paul, we beg God for healing...and sometimes He says no. But perhaps, the Lord has a better plan for us, as He did for Paul.

In Paul's case, God's purpose was to keep him from pride, to help Paul experience His constantly sufficient grace to humbly keep going, and to show God's power through Paul's weakness (2 Corinthians 12:9).

God's answer for us also might be His sufficient grace. Our thorns may be here to stay, but He encourages us with this verse:

"Therefore, preparing your minds for action, and being sober-minded, set your hope fully on the grace that will be brought to you at the revelation of Jesus Christ" (I Peter 1:13 ᴇsᴠ). Maybe our illness is a "thorn" to help us place our hope completely on the day we will see Jesus, by His grace.

Let's pray for healing, but also trust His grace so we might be able to sing, "Amazing grace, how sweet the sound" ("Amazing Grace," Newton, J., 1779).

Do you have a song of trust you could sing today?

-Lauri Hogle

———————— *Notes & Prayers* ————————

THOSE MOMENTS CALLED UNCOMFORTABLE

My son, do not despise or be weary of his reproof,
for the Lord reproves him whom he loves,
as a father the son in whom he delights.
Proverbs 3:11–12 ESV

Ever had an experience when you've been sure you were doing everything right...and then someone points out you aren't? It's not a warm, fuzzy experience. It can be downright shocking if you never saw it coming. What to do in those moments?

Our first response could be, "Hey wait a minute! I didn't do anything to deserve this!" Then, we could go off on a tirade, defending ourselves whole-heartedly. Or we could consider the source inferior writing it off as quickly as it happened. And then there is a third tactic.

We could take it all in and ask God to divulge any revelation He has to offer. Whether we defend ourselves or not, whether the source is credible to us or not, God has allowed the moment. Perhaps this means there is growth for one or both people in the conflict. Even if we believe we are blameless, it is our duty to step aside and let God assume His role as Vindicator in the situation. It doesn't mean we should be doormats for anyone who has a desire to trample our character or behavior. But the conflict process must include seeking God quietly before we automatically go on the defensive.

We can explore the matter in prayer before exhibiting a reaction—even if that includes staying silent until we have had some alone time to sort things out with Him. Most encounters do not require immediate replies. It's perfectly okay to say, "I need to think this through and will get back to you."

Our willingness to submit ourselves to an uncomfortable moment may also include the realization that it may take some time to feel comfortable again. In the end, we must accept there are some things requiring trust in God to rectify that which needs to be made whole again.

How did you approach your last uncomfortable moment? What response could have made it better?

–Melanie Stiles

Notes & Prayers

WHAT COULD JOB DO?

*Dress for action like a man; I will question you
and you make it known to me.*
Job 40:7 ESV

The book of Job is filled with treasures for the Christian. Its perspective is almost too wide to comprehend. But one question may be important to ponder: What could Job have done to improve his situation? We know he had lost everything in life. His health included. Did God say, "Come on, try a bit harder. Pull yourself together. Don't just lie there in that ash heap. Cheer up, man!"?

No, not at all. Job needed to learn to listen to God. God would take care of the rest. God would take responsibility for Job's future. God began to explain to Job that His thoughts were a lot higher than human thinking. Job should not focus on things too difficult for him to fathom. Questions like, Why is this happening to me?

God does not speak to Job as if he was some pitiful character surrounded by miserable conditions. God treats him as a responsible person and says to him: You answer me now, answer like a man. God raises Job into a position where he can interact. And humbly Job admits he had not understood God. We do not see Job as a useless man whose life is over.

How could we remember this the next time we suffer from physical pains and feel useless in the middle of exhaustion? When suffering brings questions to the surface, do as Job did. Listen to God. He has our futures firmly in His hands. Trust what lies ahead of you to the One Who knows and understands.

–Anu Ahonen

THE POWER IS IN THE COMMAND

Have I not commanded you? Be strong and courageous!
Do not tremble or be dismayed, for the Lord your
God is with you wherever you go.
Joshua 1:9 NASB

As we go through the journey of life, we may encounter many bumps and ruts along the way. These could be from losses we've faced, illnesses, or other challenges which have come into our lives. We may face times of fear and despair when we feel all is lost.

There is good news. If Christ is your Savior, you don't need to be afraid of anything life throws at you. God commanded us to not be afraid or dismayed. Why did He give this command? There are scary things in the world. He says this because He is always with us. If God is constantly with us as He says He is, there is no need for fear. He gives us the strength to face anything He allows in our lives. Even better, wherever we go, He goes with us. He never leaves us alone (Hebrews 13:5).

When we choose to trust Him, He gives us courage. He helps us fight the battles we go through. We can stand strong and courageous in Him. There is no reason for us to tremble or be dismayed. He would not command us to do something if it were impossible. With the command comes the strength through Him. With strength comes courage. Our God is on our side, and He fights along with us. What a blessing and a comfort!

Are you feeling afraid right now because of a challenge you are facing? Do you feel like there's no hope? God is right there with you. Call out to Him in prayer for strength and courage.

–Julie Wilson Smith

TILL IT UNTIL IT'S HEALED

For we are God's fellow workers;
you are God's field, God's building.
1 Corinthians 3:9 NASB

Consider this parable. Once, there was a vast field replete with weeds so tall that some grew into what looked like trees. One day, the landowner approached the nightmare of a field donned in clothing prepared for hard work. Thankfully, the irrigation system made the ground soft and pliable. Even a tall weed could be pulled out with little effort.

As the owner pulled a foot-long weed out, she figured the method she had applied was easiest, so she pulled, pulled, and pulled. She discovered that the root of the small weed was more than six feet long with other much larger weeds attached. She realized what she thought were many individual weeds was actually a one-weed-root system. It had overtaken the entire yard. The reality of one weed permeating the entire field was stunning to her.

Our bodies are like that field. The strong winds of life's cares, the blight of persecution, or the pestilence of disease often creates underground systems that seem to ravage the field that is our body. But the Lord wants us to take part in tilling the ground of our hearts until healing is achieved. This work, this tilling, is an act of worship by caring for the gift God gave us.

We tend to remember that Jesus instructed us to love our neighbor, but forget the part which says, "as we love ourselves." This means to show ourselves some loving care so we can share that same level of love with others. Don't feel guilty for pampering yourself from time to time.

Ponder ways you can practically till the field of your body and measures you can take to promote relief, rest, and restoration. Then, implement those measures. In the spirit of worship, begin to give the body Your Father entrusted to you extra care, believing in faith that one day, you will receive a reward for the fruits of your labor. In doing so, you will position your field to be tilled and healed.

-Sharon Williams

— Notes & Prayers —

LIKE THE DEER

GOD, the Lord, is my strength;
he makes my feet like the deer's;
he makes me tread on my high places.
Habakkuk 3:19 ESV

In the beautiful Pacific Northwest of the United States, the sight of a deer is a common occurrence. They are some of the most remarkable animals God has created. Though deer can get fairly large, they remain agile and swift, moving surefooted over mountainous terrain and leaping over obstacles more than twelve-feet high. They are unafraid and confident as they easily scale the heights. These traits of deer have been used several times in the Bible to describe parts of one's spiritual journey.

Habakkuk's confidence and faith in the Lord are evident in today's verse. He wholeheartedly relied on God for strength. Habakkuk's trust in the Lord was so great he said He made his feet like those of a deer. This was appropriate considering the terrible difficulties he faced. The impending invasion of the Babylonians left Habakkuk trembling, but he held strong to his faith in the Lord which made him surefooted and able to avoid obstacles in his path. This allowed him to reach the spiritual high places where he could commune with God.

We all encounter difficulties or trials that, in our human power, cause us to stumble, block our path, or bring us to a place of fear. Living with chronic pain or illness can be the cause of these difficulties, making it challenging to feel the Lord's presence with us, and like Habakkuk, we can declare God as our strength as we move forward to the other side of the trial and on to our high places. We may not fully understand how much God has been our strength until later when we look back at our experiences and see all of the times, He kept us from falling.

As you encounter difficulties today, lean on the strength of the Lord knowing He will keep you from stumbling as you trust Him.

–Jodine Zeitler

Notes & Prayers

GOD KNOWS YOUR NAME

Then she called the name of The LORD who spoke to her,
"You are a God who sees."
Genesis 16:13a NASB

One of the most difficult parts of living with chronic illness is hiddenness. A person can look fine to an observer, while on the inside, their body is trying to destroy itself. Sadness, loneliness, and lack of understanding can lead to the feeling of being invisible. Unseen. Unheard. Unloved.

A woman of the Bible knew those feelings. In the hardest part of her life, Hagar ran from a situation where she could have felt used and unimportant. Physically and emotionally, she sought to escape from what she thought was an unbearable situation. She ended up by a spring of water in the wilderness.

An angel of the Lord came to her, which means God saw her. He saw what she'd gone through. He saw her heartache. He saw her fears. And He called her by name.

Have you ever felt like you were in a wilderness? Alone? Scared? Not knowing what to do? The situation may be different, but the feelings are the same. Sometimes, the simple reminder of being visible is the sweetest reality.

Remember, God knows what you're going through. On those days when it seems no one understands, hears, or sees, He does. When you have to keep pushing through, and you look fine but inside you're not, God is with you. In those moments, when all you want is for someone to react with compassion and not with a comment like, "but you look fine," God knows. He understands what you mean when someone asks how you are, and you say, "I'm fine," when, with everything in you, what you want to say is, "If you only knew." He does.

If possible, spend some time today listening to or reading Genesis 16 and let it encourage you. You are not alone. God is right there with you through every moment of loneliness. God sees you and He cares. He knows your name (Isaiah 43:1; John 10:3).

-Susan Sage

— *Notes & Prayers* —

STILL SALTY

You are the salt of the earth, but if salt has lost its taste, how shall its saltiness be restored? It is no longer good for anything except to be thrown out and trampled under people's feet.
Matthew 5:13 ESV

Did you know sprinkling a pineapple with salt makes it taste sweeter? Table salt is mainly sodium chloride and is effective in lowering bitterness levels in some foods. It diminishes our tongue's perception of sour tastes caused by acidity. While this information tidbit is interesting, in biblical times, salt was valued differently.

In the Sermon on the Mount, Jesus referred to the fishermen, shepherds, and other laborers listening to Him as the salt of the earth. With His help, they were the preservative that could overcome the acidic enemy of the world. He considered them worthy and virtuous enough to die on the cross to redeem.

In those days, salt was so valuable it was used as a form of commerce, right beside other currencies. Roman soldiers were known to have been paid with salt. The Latin word for salt is "sal," from which the word "salary" is derived.

Jesus was implying His followers were a great commodity. He hasn't changed His opinion about believers today. He still considers us His partners, working through us to accomplish His will on earth. And He will continue to do so until His Son returns. The question to consider is this: "How do we see ourselves?"

In a world that makes it easy to devalue each other, we should strive to return to what Jesus thinks about us. His opinion never changes, and we can stand in agreement with Him daily.

The next time you take a glance at yourself in the mirror, let the Lord know you are aware of how He values you. Simply say aloud, for both Him and you to hear, "Lord, I'm still sassy, salty, and ready to serve You!"

–Melanie Stiles

Notes & Prayers

UNOFFENDED

And blessed is the one who is not offended by me.
Matthew 11:6 ESV

Jesus did not behave according to people's expectations. The Jews were hoping for Him to be the king that would set them free from Roman rule. The disciples were expecting Jesus to be the triumphant Messiah. But what did Jesus prove to be like, according to the biblical record?

The New Testament tells us people thronged to hear Him. They also brought their sick to be healed and their children to be blessed. And Jesus healed the sick and blessed the children. But He wanted to do more. He had compassion for the people who gathered to Him, who He saw as lost like sheep without a shepherd. He wanted them to understand that He was their Good Shepherd who would search for the lost sheep and bring them to a place of shelter. He would carry the weak lambs in His arms and feed the hungry. To those parched with thirst, He would give living water.

As a Christian walks with Jesus, it may sometimes seem that Jesus is different from what He was at the beginning of their relationship with Him. Complicated situations arise in life and we do not always easily understand what we should do or how to respond. Even though we feel that Jesus may not be as we originally thought, He is still the same Good Shepherd we followed. He still refreshes the weary and gives strength to the weak (Isaiah 40:29).

Jesus came to save all humankind from the power of darkness. It was something so unfathomably great that people could not take it in. Isaiah reminds us that God's thoughts about us are quite different from what we human beings can even suspect; they are higher as the heavens are higher than the earth (Isaiah 55:8–9).

When we feel disappointed that God has not done something as we wanted, it is important to remember His ways are higher and better. Take your disappointment to God and invite Him to speak to you through them.

–Anu Ahonen

———— *Notes & Prayers* ————

GOD IS NEAR

*The Lord your God is in your midst, a victorious
warrior. He will exult over you with joy,
He will be quiet in His love, He will rejoice
over you with shouts of joy.*
Zephaniah 3:17 NASB

Walking through this life of pain and suffering, either our own or a loved one's may leave us feeling alone and isolated. We may be surrounded by other patients or family members, yet still, feel disconnected. Perhaps we wonder if it's worth the fight.

"The Lord your God is in your midst," says Zephaniah. The Lord is with us as we travel the path we're on. He's with us in the middle of all the pain and suffering. He's a victorious warrior Who is on our side as we fight. God doesn't leave us to struggle alone.

God loves each of us so much, that He rejoices over us with joy. He's happy and elated with us, no matter the faults or fears. He is right beside us, cheering us on with shouts of joy. Can you imagine the booming voice of God calling your name and saying, "You can do it!"? He is present with you and He cares when you feel alone, and when you feel like you're fighting a losing battle with no hope in sight.

Through the hard days when the suffering seems unbearable, remember, God is present with you. He is fighting for you. He's on your side; cheering you on. God's love is also quiet. It's soothing to the soul. It's comforting. No words need to be spoken. There's a feeling of total acceptance and peace. Rest in the peace of His love.

-Julie Wilson Smith

HOW ARE YOU?

Casting all your anxieties on him, because he cares for you.
1 Peter 5:7 ESV

"Hello. How are you?" The most common greeting of our age—in any language, this is often the first thing we hear or say when we come into contact with someone. We typically hear simple responses like, "I'm fine." Quite ironic.

Then there are those believers who are taught to always speak blessings over the lives of others. From them, we hear things like, "Blessed" and "Highly favored." But how many times are we only saying this by faith, or as some would say, "Faking it until we make it?"

Wouldn't it be nice just for once to be able to say something like, "I'm not so great today," or, "I'm having a rough time these days," without feeling like we'll be judged, or that people won't soon tire of our so-called pessimistic attitude?

Unfortunately, many people don't really care how the person they greet is doing. The question is simply one of common courtesy. Sometimes, wouldn't we like to say, "Don't bother asking if you don't want to know the answer?" This might be what we wish we could say, but it might not endear us to many people.

Today, please entertain this question. Answer it according to how you feel physically, emotionally, or spiritually. Feel free to express exactly how you feel at this very moment. If you want to vent, then vent.

But before you begin, start your statement with these words, "Precious Father, I'm so glad to know You care about how I'm feeling today. I thank You that You will not judge how I feel, and so here it goes..." Now, begin to tell Him exactly how you are feeling today.

If you are feeling wonderful, celebrate Him for that blessing. If you are in pain, thank Him for His promise to carry your burdens with a gentle "Hallelujah, anyhow." If you are worn out and tired, thank Him for His promise to give you rest. He cares, and He does want to know.

-Sharon Williams

Notes & Prayers

STEADFAST UNDER TRIAL

Blessed is the man who remains steadfast under trial, for when he has stood the test he will receive the crown of life, which God has promised to those who love him.
James 1:12 ESV

Many of the trials we encounter in our lives are short-term problems or temptations requiring a burst of fortitude to withstand. However, some trials do not end quickly, if ever. For those of us who struggle with chronic pain and conditions, we know all too well about trials with no apparent end. It is grueling to endure pain and illness day after day making it easy to lose hope and become bitter about the situations we face.

James tells us we will be blessed and receive the crown of life if we remain steadfast under trial. To be steadfast is to stand firm or not waver. Therefore, we are to have unwavering faith in God, even in the face of all kinds of trials. A person who determinedly and consistently faces their trials with devotion to God will be blessed and receive the crown of life. The crown of life may not refer to the gift of salvation but could be an additional reward we would receive in heaven, or it could be the idea of life being more abundant here on earth because of our steadfastness. Whichever way, the reward is worth our intentional endeavors to persevere and trust God even during the difficult trials we face.

As you face trials today, don't lose trust in God Who loves you and wants every good thing for you. Ask God to help you remain steadfast and believe in Him for His promises.

–Jodine Zeitler

THANK YOU, GOD

Oh come, let us sing to the LORD; let us make
a joyful noise to the rock of our salvation!
Psalm 95:2 ESV

A hymn written in 1636 encourages us to sing, "Now thank we all our God with heart and hands and voices" ("Now Thank We All Our God," Rinkart, M., 1636). But what if our bodies are drowning in agony, our minds swirling in stress, and our hearts exploding with sorrow? How can we possibly sing with a joyful noise? How can we have a heart of gratefulness and thank God?

"Rejoice always, pray without ceasing, give thanks in all circumstances; for this is the will of God in Christ Jesus for you" (1 Thessalonians 5:16–18 ESV). All does mean "all." God does not say feel thanks in all circumstances. He says it's His will for us to give thanks. To give is to offer, acknowledge, and consider another person.

Giving happens in relationships; it's an outward and purposeful act of love for another. Giving thanks comes from God because we are in Christ Jesus. By His indwelling Spirit, we can rejoice and sing thanks as a gift. For what could we thank God?

We can sing, "Thank You, God" for salvation. Our agony doesn't change what He's done for us in the gospel. "Christ died for our sins in accordance with the Scriptures, that he was buried, that he was raised on the third day in accordance with the Scriptures" (1 Corinthians 15: 3–4 ESV). Our stress doesn't change His truth that for believers in Christ, "this light and momentary affliction is preparing for us an eternal weight of glory beyond all comparison (2 Corinthians 4:17 ESV). Our sorrow is held by the One Who will in the coming ages..."show the immeasurable riches of his grace in kindness toward us in Christ Jesus" (Ephesians 2:7 ESV).

Although our pain may not produce immediate emotions of gratitude, we can indeed say, "Thank You, God." Our "Thank You" words often respond to Jesus and His love. Then, joy often grows!

What are your "Thank You" words today?

-Lauri Hogle

Notes & Prayers

SEND THE VOICES AWAY

Again He stooped down and wrote on the ground.
When they heard it, they began to go out one by one,
beginning with the older ones, and He was left alone,
and the woman where she was, in the center of the court.
John 8:8–9

Have you ever replayed a conversation in your head to discover where it went wrong, or created a made-up discussion in your mind, attempting to defend yourself against someone's accusations? When we find we are not able to articulate our defense in the exact moment, we might do those things.

Our world is full of those who would declare us guilty over many factors. But only God knows the complete truth. He recognizes whether there is any foundation for claims. He knows the motives for the finger-pointing.

The devil is good at finding opportunities to set believers up and get us to bear blame whether correct or not. The voices he uses are often loud, obnoxious, rude, and can be surprising.

Jesus stepped between the woman who had been accused of adultery and her persecutors. He silenced the voices by writing something on the ground for all to see, then He said, "He who is without sin among you, let him be the first to throw a stone at her" (John 8:7b).

He does the same for us. He inserts Himself between us and the devil's indictments. But we have to allow it. The woman didn't stop Jesus. Why would she? He was there to help her, so of course, she accepted the unexpected.

Do we? Or do we allow the past experiences of defeat to stay in a loop repeating the allegations? Do we create scenarios in our thoughts where we would have known exactly what to say? Instead of making us feel better, these actions can drive the incrimination deeper into our hearts resulting in the opposite of what we hoped.

God desires to silence condemning voices. When the voices grow loud, turn to God's Word for help. Read Romans 8 aloud and let God speak His absolute truth.

–Susan Sage

Notes & Prayers

THE PEACE OF JESUS

Peace I leave with you; my peace I give to you.
Not as the world gives do I give to you.
Let not your hearts be troubled, neither let them be afraid.
John 12:27 ESV

John, the gospel writer, recorded for us the farewell speech Jesus gave to His disciples. That speech holds a very special tone, every word seems weighty. First and foremost, Jesus wanted His friends not to be overcome with fear.

Why was there no cause to be fearful even if Jesus was leaving them? Up to that point, they had been with Jesus daily and the thought of Him leaving shocked and troubled them. Jesus told them He was giving them a gift. They would get the very best He had to give: His own peace. He would send them the Holy Spirit, the Helper and Advocate, who would also bring peace.

"My peace I give to you," Jesus said. It didn't, and still doesn't, come from anywhere or anyone else. It passes understanding and is beyond any previous experience. And what were the first words Jesus uttered when He appeared to the disciples after His death and resurrection? "Peace to you."

The apostle Paul linked prayer and peace with each other. He advised us to leave every concern in prayer to God (Philippians 4:6–7). We are to bring every single thing that causes helplessness—every fear, every worry—to Him Then the Holy Spirit can bring peace and will guard our hearts. His peace will be ours as we practice this.

Where do you need peace today? Look for verses in Scripture concerning the subject of your need. Take those concerns to God, then allow Him to speak peace into your heart through His Word.

–Anu Ahonen

Notes & Prayers

YOU'RE IN GOD'S THOUGHTS

How precious are Your thoughts to me, O God!
How vast is the sum of them!
Psalms 139:17 NASB

Do you ever wake up in the morning and are unable to perform even the simplest task because of pain and fatigue? Everything takes too much energy.

Family and friends don't understand, even though they may try. "You don't look sick," they tell you. "Certainly, you can come with us today. It will do you good to get out of the house," they say.

You would genuinely like to go, but your body rebels, so you stay home alone again. As tears well up in your eyes, threatening to spill over any minute, do you feel all alone as the darkness surrounds you?

Be encouraged. You are not alone. You never have been and never will be. If you have Jesus as your Lord, He is always with you. God thinks about you constantly and is always by your side. He tenderly envelopes you in His arms and holds you close as the tears fall. He holds you tightly as you fall asleep. He is there when you awake.

Today's verse reminds us that there is no limit or any way to count how many times God thinks about us in a day, much less over a lifetime. Isn't that a comforting thought? He cares. We are precious to Him; each one individually.

When pain and fatigue come, remind yourself of God's care. Remember, He is thinking about you. Thank Him for His constant presence. Bask in His love. By choosing to focus on how much

God loves you, the struggles may be a bit easier to bear. Can you imagine that God cares for you that much?

How can you incorporate this verse so you will feel His presence? Read it, inserting your name, and think about His great love for you.

–Julie Wilson Smith

Notes & Prayers

UNLIKELY VESSELS

Now when they saw the boldness of Peter and John, and
perceived that they were uneducated, common men,
they were astonished. And they recognized that
they had been with Jesus.
Acts 4:13 ESV

When you examine the lives and characters of the people God chose to use in Scripture, do you ever ask yourself why God chose them? What set them apart? What made them the "chosen" leaders? Would you vote for them in an election if you knew their story?

In Exodus, we meet Moses, a murderer who fled his homeland to spare his life. He tried to convince God he was not qualified to do what God planned for him because of a speech impediment. Yet God chose him to lead an entire nation out of captivity.

In Joshua chapter 2, we find Rahab, a prostitute in a pagan land—someone deemed unclean by society. Yet God used her to help Israel conquer Jericho. She even became an ancestor of the Messiah (Matthew 1:5).

In John 4, we read of a Samaritan woman who was living with a man after being married seven times. Even though she remained nameless, God used her to become what many people consider the first evangelist after she told her entire village about Jesus.

In Judges 11, we learn of Jephthah, the son of a prostitute disowned by his own family. Why would God have chosen him to deliver His people from the hands of the Ammonites?

None of these people were likely vessels, but they all were given an assignment from God.

We each have an assignment. Many people may struggle with what God gives us to do because their judgment blinds them due

to what they "think" they see. But we must hold fast to our faith. Remember God promised to complete the work He started in us.

Don't be afraid to declare His work in you. You are indeed an unlikely vessel, one He appointed, one He commissioned. So, despite what others may think or say, freely and unashamedly fulfill your commission in the name of Jesus.

-Sharon Williams

— Notes & Prayers —

WAYPOINTS TO REDEMPTION

And after you have suffered a little while, the God of all grace, who has called you to His eternal glory in Christ, will Himself restore, confirm, strengthen, and establish you.
1 Peter 5:10 ESV

In its various forms, in one way or another, suffering is something we all live with. For those of us with chronic pain and conditions, it is a common occurrence. Suffering may be a result of sin or used to discipline and train us to combat sin. Sometimes it occurs as a result of us standing for what is right. Sometimes we willingly suffer by giving up our comfort, time, or possessions to serve others.

There may be times when difficulties linger as we wait for an answer to prayer. Though it is not fun, it hurts, and may not seem fair, suffering is part of the Christian life that produces righteousness and peace. Whatever the circumstances, as believers, we can hold tightly to the knowledge that what we endure on earth is temporary, the Holy Spirit will help us to withstand as we wait for His deliverance.

The hardships of our suffering on earth are waypoints along our road to redemption. We know this because our gracious God, from whom we receive unmerited favor, has provided a path to salvation through our Savior, Jesus Christ. When we are called into His eternal glory in heaven, God Himself restores, confirms, strengthens, and establishes us. Our suffering will be no more because we will be made perfect, as He created us to be. It is because of this assurance of eternal glory with our Heavenly Father that we can view the painful circumstances of this world, and these imperfect bodies positively.

Whatever you are dealing with today, remember that this temporary suffering is just that—temporary compared to the eternal glory that awaits you. When discouragement hits, ask God to show you a verse that will lift your heart to see Him.

-Jodine Zeitler

Notes & Prayers

TAKE HEART, IT'S ME

But when the disciples saw him walking on the sea,
they were terrified, and said,
"It is a ghost!" and they cried out in fear.
Matthew 14:26 ESV

In the beginning, God created a fear-free world. Can you imagine? Adam and Eve felt no fear but walked freely in intimate safety with each other and God. But since Genesis 3, fear permeates our sinful world.

The disciples felt terror when they didn't recognize Jesus. They couldn't imagine that kind of power. Men can't walk on the sea! They thought He must be a ghost. How could this man have authority over the natural order of creation? The answer? Jesus is and was fully God and fully man.

What happened next? "But immediately Jesus spoke to them, saying, "Take heart; it is I. Do not be afraid." (Matthew 14:27 ESV). He spoke to settle their fear.

Who speaks to us, when we're afraid? Jesus, the I AM. Jesus, who sustains and upholds the entire universe. Jesus, King of kings and Lord of lords. Jesus, who died in our place so we would be given His righteousness in place of our sin. Jesus, our beautiful Savior.

In this fallen world, fear may grip our hearts when our illnesses boil over into a potential crisis. But our Savior speaks to us by His Word. He says to us in our suffering, "I have said these things to you, that in me you may have peace. In the world you will have tribulation. But take heart, I have overcome the world" (John 16:33 ESV).

As we wait for the day when He restores all things to fear-free perfection in the new heaven and earth (Revelation 21), let's take heart. What song focuses your heart on the power of Jesus, when your heart is afraid? Let's sing today as we prepare our hearts for those crisis days of fear.

-Lauri Hogle

Notes & Prayers

WHILE WE ARE WAITING

He put another parable before them, saying,
"The kingdom of heaven is like a grain of mustard
seed that a man took and sowed in his field."
Matthew 13:31 ESV

In our drive-thru, one-click world, the art of having patience tends to get lost. No longer do we wait for merchandise until we have saved enough to pay for it. We can whip out a credit card. We've even been supplied with the option of taking a "rapid" Covid test, instead of waiting three days for results from the standard molecular test. Consequently, waiting can be very frustrating for the average person, especially when it comes to those things we have prayed about.

Yet God could be allowing us to wait for a variety of reasons. He could simply be re-teaching us the act of living in His grace with a good attitude, despite not getting what we want exactly when we want it. Jesus compares the Kingdom of Heaven to a seed. From our own experience, we have seen that an acorn, given enough time, will grow into a mighty oak. Hence, God's plans for our lives might require patience.

We can see how much Jesus loves us by how patient He is with our lives as He works in us to do good, even if what He is asking us to seems unthinkable. Consider Abraham in the Old Testament. Abraham loved and trusted God, even when he was told to sacrifice Isaac.

Our journey may also include going through some hard places where our true hearts can be revealed. We are in the right attitude when we can honestly say, "Lord, I want these things, but none of them is worth trading my relationship with You. You are truly all I need."

God wants us to stand in His presence and wait patiently before His throne. He prefers we come to Him with thanksgiving, even if we are still waiting for our prayers to be answered. When we feel the strain of impatience, it might be wise to remember we are not the first. Moses waited forty years to lead the Israelites out of Egypt.

How well are you waiting?

–Melanie Stiles

Notes & Prayers

WHAT ABUNDANCE?

The thief comes only to steal and kill and destroy;
I came that they may have life, and have it abundantly.
John 10:10 NASB

Have you ever had something stolen from you? Did the event leave you shaken, untrusting, and dismayed? This is exactly what the devil wants as he tries to steal our joy and attempts to shake our faith.

Jesus said He came to not only give us life in Him but came so we could live that life abundantly. We might also think of it as richly and lavishly. It is possible though that with abundance in mind, we could get the wrong idea of what it means. To our culture, abundance means numerous possessions: houses, boats, cars, computers, jewels, property, and more—everything money can buy.

For God, abundance means Him. Hebrews 7:25(ESV) says,"Consequently, He is able to save to the uttermost those who draw near to God through him, since he always lives to make intercession for them." In our spiritual life, uttermost means completely and perfectly. Nothing left out. It is the same idea as abundance.

When we are in the middle of an illness cycle, life can feel anything but complete, perfect, or abundant. We want to enjoy family, friends, and activities and not be too sick to think about a fulfilled life.

In those moments, God reaches out to remind us His abundance is still available. He gives peace—an inner stillness when storms rage; joy—the deep acknowledgment of who God is and all He's done; hope—the ability to look beyond the moment; and serenity—a hidden, mysterious faith in God's sovereignty.

These are but a few of the abundant treasures within our reach, no matter what our current circumstances might be.

As God's children, we can live in the abundance of His love, forgiveness, strength, joy, faithfulness, gentleness, and much more because He never changes and His promises are forever true. If possible, spend some time today making a list of blessings God has given you. Keep the list close by. Practice recognizing the abundance of God.

-Susan Sage

Notes & Prayers

THE LORD DOES GREAT THINGS FOR US

The Lord has done great things for us; we are glad.
Psalms 126:3 NASB

When the global illness, COVID-19, was at its strongest, many people were hospitalized due to respiratory symptoms. Some of these had to be put on a ventilator to breathe. Life and death hung in the balance. Today's verse above certainly could describe the feelings of those patients and their families.

God does great things for us every day. They might not be this dramatic, but they are still great. We just need to open our eyes to see them. Have you ever sat at the beach and observed a beautiful sunrise or sunset? What about the tiny designs in snowflakes? No two are exactly alike. God gives us the beauty of nature every day.

What about the great things that are closer to us? Holding a newborn baby for the first time. Hearing the laughter of a child. Spending time with aging parents or grandparents. Listening to their wisdom. Friends who encourage us and walk through life with us. All of these are gifts from a loving God for us to enjoy. And His salvation is the biggest gift of all. God has done so much for us. We need to live a life of gratitude and awareness so we don't take them for granted. Let's keep our eyes open to God's blessings with a thankful heart. May we be amazed at all He does for us and be glad.

What are some of the blessings God has given? Think about the small gifts as well as the big ones. A good exercise is to write them down so when we become discouraged, we can look back at the list and receive another blessing from each one.

–Julie Wilson Smith

THE BEAUTY OF BROKENNESS

And He took the five loaves and the two fish,
and looking up toward heaven, He blessed the food and broke
the loaves and He kept giving them to the disciples to set
before them, and He divided up the two fish among them all.
They all ate and were satisfied, and they picked up twelve
full baskets of the broken pieces, and also the fish.
Mark 6:41–43 NASB

Just think: Jesus was able to feed thousands of people with a two-piece fish dinner! Now that's a miracle! But there's more to the story than the buffet miracle. Notice what it took for the masses to become satiated. First Jesus blessed the food, then He broke it. Only then could there be enough to go around.

Jesus didn't stop by proving that He could provide sustenance for them. And neither does He stop proving His provision for us. Let's consider Him—the Bread of Life. Indeed, He was blessed. His aunt Elizabeth acknowledged the fact before He was even born. Yet while Jesus was on earth in human form, He was limited because He could only be in one place at a time. The only way Jesus could give everyone access to Himself simultaneously was to allow Himself to be broken, and that He did indeed! He allowed Himself to be scourged, spat upon, whipped mercilessly, crowned with thorns, and crucified between criminals.

Had Jesus not allowed Himself to be blessed by the Father and then broken by man, His Spirit would not have been released and poured out on all flesh, and we would not be partakers of the goodness of the infilling of God's Spirit today.

This may be tough to grasp, but if we feel broken, embrace it. This is the Potter's way of putting us back together in a manner befitting royalty so that there can be enough of you to fulfill God's purpose for your life. By embracing brokenness, you will begin to appreciate the beauty within the new you.

Where do you need to be broken today? Ask God to show you.

–Sharon Williams

—— *Notes & Prayers* ——

EYES STRAIGHT AHEAD

Let your eyes look directly ahead
And let your gaze be fixed straight in front of you.
Proverbs 4:25 NASB

Have you ever seen the blinders horses often wear to keep them from seeing anything other than what is directly in front of them? Horses get distracted easily so wearing the blinders reduces their field of vision helping them stay focused on their tasks. Racehorses also wear blinders to keep their focus on the race. Maybe we, like horses, need blinders.

Our world is filled with chaos and distractions that can easily pull our attention away from the things on which we need to focus. We may be full of fear, constantly looking around for harmful, dangerous things. We can lose our focus on our spiritual race and grow stagnant or even regress.

Proverbs 4:25 encourages us to keep our eyes looking directly ahead of us at the right things. This verse follows two that tell us to be careful about our heart's passions and to be careful how we speak. These encouragements will help us avoid temptations, distractions, and unnecessary stress.

Another reason to keep our eyes set on what is in front of us is so we will look straight ahead at those we encounter. By keeping our eyes on others, we have a better chance of seeing their needs and perhaps being in a better position to help them.

Put on your "blinders" today to remain focused on what God has for you.

–Jodine Zeitler

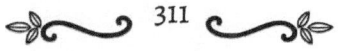

SHOW ME YOUR GLORY

Moses said, "Please show me your glory."
Exodus 33:18 ESV

God led Moses into scary, overwhelming, unknown territory, way out of his comfort zone, dependent on God's grace for every moment. We understand Moses's fears. Chronic illness feels like this to us, especially when we need to continue caring for others and fulfilling responsibilities.

Moses needed to see God's glory ... and so do we. God showered him with grace, with His glorious presence. Let's consider ways to see God's glory. The Lord said to Moses, "I know you by name" (Exodus 33:17 ESV). Beloved, He knows us by name too (John 10:3). He knows every intricate cell and process in our body. Each day of life, He knows our thoughts, needs, desires, and sins, and knew them all before we were born (Psalm 139). Can you see His glory in His vast, powerful, infinite knowing?

When the sickbed consumes our vision and fears arise, maybe we need to see our Creator's glory. Even a picture will do. Can you see anything beautiful in nature or around you? "The heavens declare the glory of God and the sky above proclaims his handiwork" (Psalm 19:1 ESV).

Singing to our glorious God may be helpful as well. He's shown us His grace and love by giving us "knowledge of the glory of God in the face of Jesus Christ" (2 Corinthians 4:6 ESV). When we sing to our Lord, glorifying Him, praising Him, He reminds us of His glory, even as we do this from the sickbed. And one day, we will see the glory of the Lord with an unveiled face (2 Corinthians 3:18). This sickness may help carry us into beholding Him on that day.

So today, let's ask Him to show us His glory now as we hold onto hope. Let's sing, "Fairest Lord Jesus, Ruler of all nature, Thou, my soul's glory, joy, and crown" ("Fairest Lord Jesus," anon., 1677).

What could you do to actively see God's glory today?

-Lauri Hogle

———— *Notes & Prayers* ————

REFRESHING PRAYER

*Praying at all times in the Spirit, with all prayer
and supplication. To that end, keep alert with all
perseverance, making supplication for all the saints.*
Ephesians 6:18 ESV

No matter the condition of our bodies, we have, in our singular possession, the most powerful spiritual weapon in existence. The ability to pray. Yet, in the heat of our battles on earth, we can lose sight of how imperative this simple act is in determining change.

Everyone has experienced struggling with prayer. What should I pray for? My prayers feel repetitive and stale. It's in these moments that we can go back to the basics and, consequently, rejuvenate how we seek our Father in Heaven.

We can start by praising God for Who He is. Praying the Names of God is a way we can reconnect with His omniscience and magnificence. Next, we can thank God for what He has done, not only in our own lives but for giving His only Son in sacrifice for us. Then we can take our prayer viewpoint off ourselves and pray solely for others. We can lift those we know who are in need. We can add prayers for our cities, nations, and all leaders. We mustn't overlook praying for all who do not yet know Jesus as Lord. And finally, we can pray to be able to love and bless the people we find difficult to love.

Changing the focus of our prayers is a sure way to alter and refresh our daily approach to God. Stepping away from our old routine opens the door for God to make us aware of circumstances and conditions we might otherwise have ignored. This, in turn, can create a new zeal for pressing into prayer.

When is the last time you reinvigorated your prayer life? Should it be today?

–Melanie Stiles

THE GOD WHO RESPONDS

Turn to me and be gracious to me,
for I am lonely and afflicted.
Psalm 25:16 NASB

Alone again. Stuck in bed. No chance for social interactions. Too weary to text, call, or open social media. Loneliness can weigh heavily, no matter what we're going through, but especially during those cycles of illness where no end is visible. Maybe the question even arises: Is this all there will ever be?

God responded with compassion to people in the Bible who knew the same type of lonesomeness. Hagar sat alone in the desert twice. God saw her. She called Him El Roi—"the God who sees" (Genesis 16). With no one else around, she learned of God's care for her.

Remember the bleeding woman in the Bible? Jesus called to her through those crowding against Him. He called her "daughter" (Luke 8:43–48). This was such a great moment of life-change for her to know how God saw her.

Think about Job, one of the greatest sufferers. Yet God heard and conversed with him. Job's biggest lesson was to trust when he couldn't see or understand.

With each of these and more individuals in Scripture, we see how God looked beyond their circumstances to His truth for them. He had something greater planned for them, but it started with opening their eyes and hearts to see what was possible. Sharing a relationship with Him and learning to trust Him was of great importance to God.

Today if you are able, ask God to open your eyes to see how important you are to Him. He sees you. He knows who you are because you are His (Psalm 139). He's reaching out now waiting for your trust especially when life's challenges are hard to understand.

-Susan Sage

———————— *Notes & Prayers* ————————

Notes & Prayers

Notes & Prayers

Susan Sage

Chronic illness has taught Susan Sage a great deal about God's sovereignty. She loves praying for and encouraging others in their relationship with God. Susan writes flash fiction and devotionals.

Visit https://susansage.com/

Jodine Zeitler

Jodine Zeitler is a Spiritual Director who writes devotionals, Bible studies, and children's books. She helps others deepen their love of God and realize his love for them.

Visit http://lightsshiningbrightministries.com/

Julie Smith

Julie Smith's life has had many physical challenges. She believes God's handiwork is in everything she has faced. Julie uses her writing to minister God's love to others.

Visit https://www.butterfliesblossomsandblessings.com/

Dr. Lauri Hogle

Author, educator, church musician, and retired music therapist Dr. Lauri Hogle is the founder of a nonprofit, "Singing Christ's Hope," nurturing His hope through musical and Scriptural resources for suffering women.

Visit https://laurihogle.com/

About the Authors

Sharon Nobuhle Williams

 Best-selling author of The Nehemiah Factors: Your Pathway to Godly, Effective Leadership, Sharon Nobuhle Williams is a missionary, evangelist, and teacher. Her passion is spiritual growth and development.

Visit https://globalgrowthfactors.wordpress.com

Anu Ahonen

 Writer and watercolor painter, Anu Ahonen has suffered from chronic illness for years and knows it has been an important part of the school of patience for her.

Visit https://anuahonen.com

Melanie Stiles

 Melanie Stiles is an award–winning author and Life Coach who has accumulated hundreds of bylines in various publications. She uses her background to share joys, hardships, and other life journeys with others. Melanie believes we are better together, and works to help others become the best they can be.

Visit https://melaniestiles.com/